Volume One:
THE OUTSIDERS

THE AMERICAN IMMIGRANT

CELEBRATING THOSE WHO HELP BUILD OUR NATION

elevate

Volume One:
THE OUTSIDERS

THE AMERICAN IMMIGRANT

CELEBRATING THOSE WHO HELP BUILD OUR NATION

DICK GEPHARDT & MARK RUSSELL

WITH STEPHEN CALDWELL

elevate

Published in Boise, Idaho by Elevate,
an imprint of Elevate Publishing.

This book may be purchased in bulk for educational, business, organizational, or promotional use.

For information, please email info@elevatepub.com

Print ISBN-13: 9781945449338
eBook ISBN-13: 9781945449321

CONTENTS

DEDICATION

Dick Gephardt & Mark Russell

To all of the immigrants who have made such an enormous contribution to the United States of America.

THE MAKING OF A NATION

By Dick Gephardt

*Embracing newcomers is America's strength;
diversity is the magic that makes our nation great.*

My son and I were standing in front of a hotel in New York trying with no success to catch a cab. Then a friendly gentleman tapped me on the shoulder.

"It looks like you need a ride," he said. "I have a black car service. Can I help?"

We were late for a dinner, the clock was ticking, and it seemed like we were out of options. So we got in his car and struck up a conversation as we headed through the bustling streets of Manhattan.

Within a few blocks, we learned the driver was from Bangladesh, that he'd been in the United States for 12 years, and that he not only owned the car he was driving, but 14 others just like it. He had arrived in New York with nothing, he said, and had driven a cab for three years, often for 20 hours a day. He saved all the money he could. He wanted to provide for his family and start his own business.

"So you have kids?" I asked.

"Oh, yes," he told us. "I have three. Two are in law school, and one is in medical school."

"That's incredible," I said. "And what do you think about America?"

For this question, he stopped the car. He pulled over toward the curb, but wasn't entirely out of the traffic flow. People were honking, but he paid no attention. He needed more than words to provide his answer. He turned to us, put his hands together, and with an emotional voice said, "Thank God for America. I could not have thought of doing this in Bangladesh. It would not have entered my mind."

I've spent much of my adult life involved in politics, including nearly 30 years in Congress, so I've been blessed to travel all over this great country. I've been in every state in the Union, and I've met all kinds of people who have immigrated here from all sorts of places. They're all living their personal version of the American Dream—they are celebrities, corporate executives, stay-at-home moms, waiters and waitresses, cab drivers, athletes, doctors, small business owners, or scientists.

Once I've gotten to know them, I've often asked myself a question: "Are we better off with this person in America?" Inevitably, my answer is the same: Yes. Try it. Do you know immigrants who have had a positive influence on you or your community? I've asked that question to lots of people, and most are quick to share stories about teachers, co-workers, caregivers, and friends. Who is that for you? Are you better off because of them? Are we better off because that person is in America? I believe we are.

Personally, I've always been impressed with immigrants—their persistence, their willpower, their desire to succeed, their gratitude, and their understanding of the magical opportunity this country still presents. It's amazing to see the value they add to our country by *being here.* And, as I heard the driver's story that evening in New York, something hit me in a fresh and powerful way.

I want everybody in America to hear this story…and these kinds of stories.

As a speech major in college, l learned to speak publicly and have since delivered hundreds of speeches as a politician. One thing I've learned is that people connect with you during a speech when you share stories, not policy iteration. Stories are the best way to affect public opinion in a positive way, because they represent truth. They represent reality.

And it's what you'll find in this series of Kindle Singles. The purpose isn't to argue over how to better enforce the laws we have, or to debate what laws we need to change or what policies we should enact; it simply is to share the stories of men, women, and children who have come to this country, made it their home, and made it a better place—for them, for their families, and for all of us.

Each "single" includes eight to 10 features on the lives of immigrants, the impact they've had on America, and the impact America has had on them. You'll learn the stories of immigrants from all walks of life, with all types of religious backgrounds, who came for all sorts of reasons, and who arrived from different parts of the world. As you read them, you can ask yourself the same question: Are we better off with this person in America?

We all know America is uniquely a nation of immigrants. Unless you're a Native American, you come from a family of immigrants. In fact, if you go back far enough, even the very first residents of what's now America migrated here from somewhere else.

In 2014, the Pew Research Center said there were 42.2 million immigrants living in the United States, or 13.2 percent of our population. By 2065, that number is expected to rise to 78 million immigrants.

Other developed countries—Russia, Japan, and most nations in Western Europe—have struggled to embrace immigrants, especially refugees. Some have strict limits on immigration. In Japan, for instance, immigrants are admitted based on a points system that gives preferential treatment to professionals. And Denmark gives cash incentives to immigrants who leave if they can't assimilate into the culture.

Founded by immigrants, America has always found a way to embrace a cultural tapestry woven by unique threads from all over the world. It's also the only place I know where people arrive from somewhere else and believe they can truly belong—they believe they can be an *American.* That doesn't happen anywhere else. That achievement is one of America's greatest strengths as we continue to build the future of our nation.

Not all immigrants have been good for America, of course. But the few bad apples don't change the fact that our orchard is full of amazing fruit.

Let me tell you why. As you read these stories, I think you'll pick up on two major themes: one, the character of the immigrants and, two, the character of Americans.

Firstly, immigrants arrive in America with a tremendous desire to do whatever it takes to succeed, and with an amazing sense of gratitude.

SOURCES OF IMMIGRATION TO THE U.S., BY ERA

Era and Country	Total	%
Modern Era (1965-2015)	**58,525,000**	**100**
Mexico	16,275,000	28
China*	3,175,000	5
India	2,700,000	5
Philippines	2,350,000	4
Korea	1,725,000	3
Vietnam	1,500,000	3
Cuba	1,550,000	3
El Salvador	1,500,000	3
Former USSR	1,450,000	2
Dominican Republic	1,325,000	2
REGION TOTALS		
Latin America	29,750,000	51
South/East Asia	14,700,000	25
Europe, total	6,900,000	12
Africa/Middle East	4,550,000	8
Canada**	1,150,000	2
All other	1,450,000	2
Southern/Eastern Europe Wave (1890-1919)	**18,244,000**	**100**
Italy	3,764,000	21
Austria-Hungary	3,690,000	20
Russia & Poland	3,166,000	17
United Kingdom	1,170,000	6
Germany	1,082,000	6
Ireland***	917,000	5
REGION TOTALS		
Europe, Total	16,134,000	88
>North/West Europe	4,757,000	26
>South/East Europe	11,377,000	62
Canada	835,000	5
Latin America	551,000	3

South/East Asia	315,000	2
Africa/Middle East	332,000	2
Other/Not specified	77,000	<.05
Northern European Wave (1840-1889)	**14,314,000**	**100**
Germany	4,282,000	30
Ireland***	3,209,000	22
United Kingdom	2,586,000	18
Norway-Sweden	883,000	6
REGION TOTALS		
Europe, total,	12,757,000	89
>North/West Europe	11,700,000	82
>South/East Europe	1,058,000	7
Canada	1,034,000	7
Latin America	101,000	1
South/East Asia	293,000	2
Africa/Middle East	5,000	<0.5
Other/Not specified	124,000	1

Note: Population figures rounded to the nearest 25,000 for 1965-2015; nearest thousand for earlier waves. Data for 1965-2015 include legal and unauthorized immigrants; for 1840-1919, only legal admissions are included. *Includes Hong Kong, Taiwan and Macao. ** Includes other North America. ***Includes Northern Ireland. Persons from Puerto Rico not included.

Source: For 1965-2015, Pew Research Center estimates based on adjusted census data; for 1840-1919, Office of Immigration Statistics, Yearbook of Immigration Statistics, 2008, Table 2.

Pew Research Center

There's an Arabic adage that says, "You don't know a thing until you know its opposite." In America, immigrants see the opportunity that was absent in their native land, and they seldom take it for granted. So they work hard, they are adaptable, they have grit, and they have willpower that drives them forward. Failure is not an option.

Morad Fareed, one of the people featured in this book, is a successful entrepreneur whose parents immigrated to America from Palestine in the late 1960s. Not long ago, he was in the audience for the Broadway hit musical, *Hamilton,* when the performers summed up the character of American immigrants in one of their songs. In the scene, Alexander Hamilton, an orphan from the West Indies, meets up with the French aristocrat Lafayette prior to the Battle of Yorktown.

"Finally on the field," Hamilton sings, "we've had quite a run." Lafayette responds: "Immigrants…" And then the two shake hands and lift their voices together to finish the sentence: "We get the job done!"

"Every time they say that line," Morad said, "the whole audience stands up and claps. When they said that, it really hit home."

"That's the point," said Lin-Manuel Miranda, the son of Puerto Rican immigrants who composed the musical and stars as Hamilton. During a commencement address at the University of Pennsylvania, Lin-Manuel said the musical, and the story of Hamilton's life, "reminds us that since the beginning of the great, unfinished symphony that is our American experiment, time and time again, immigrants get the job done."[1]

I couldn't agree more.

Secondly, all of us need help to make it in life, and immigrants are no exception. So in these stories you'll also see evidence of the giving, caring character of the Americans who helped immigrants find their way.

It's easy to focus on the loudest voices in the immigration debate, but all of these stories include examples of Americans who quietly and compassionately opened their homes, their hearts, and/or their wallets to help someone in need.

And, most importantly, these stories will help us all get to know each other a little better. We'll see our families in the families of those we profile. We'll see ourselves or our neighbors in some of the people who are featured, or in the people who helped them along the way. And we'll see what can happen when Americans of great character join with immigrants of great character.

I've met thousands of Americans and experienced this many times for myself. Twice I campaigned for my party's presidential nomination, and I saw people feed, house, and care for me, my family, and our volunteers in cities all across the country. Why? Because Americans, by and large, are kind, compassionate, helpful, pragmatic people driven by strong values and a love for their nation. May that never change.

COOLING THE HOT BUTTONS

Immigration has always been controversial and difficult in America; at times it's been ugly and, sometimes, it's even been bloody.

It was difficult for Native Americans when the first European settlers arrived hundreds of years ago.

It was difficult in the 1600s when more than half a million Africans were brought to America against their will as slaves.

It was difficult in the 1800s when 4.5 million Irish, 5 million Germans (including my grandparents), and some 25,000 Chinese migrated to our shores.

It was difficult in the 1900s when social and political unrest from Vietnam to Cuba brought new waves of immigrants.

And it's difficult now.

Our nation is in a new phase, and these are uniquely challenging times. In addition to the normal strains that come with immigration—the struggles of newcomers to learn the language and the customs; the struggles of nationals to understand people who look, act, and think differently—we've experienced the pressures of a horrible economy that was triggered by the recession of 2008 and the undeniable impact that terrorism has had on our national psyche.

It is understandable that we see our current situation through eyes of trepidation, but this fear cannot replace the nature that is uniquely American. We've always been a country that has found a way to welcome and accommodate immigrants.

This edition of *The American Immigrant* features immigrants whose stories connect to some of the hot-button political issues of our day. We'll learn about immigrants who came as refugees; immigrants who are Muslim; immigrants who arrived poor, but had the determination to make a life for themselves in America; and immigrants who, at one point, were in the country illegally.

Rather than debating policy, I believe these stories will humanize the debate and hopefully de-escalate the rhetoric so we all can have a more informed view of the issues.

THE REFUGEE

INTRODUCTION

By Dick Gephardt

It's inevitable that some aspects of the first-generation immigrant experience are lost with each passing generation. The flip side, however, is that each new generation has the opportunity to add something to the next—to build upon what was passed down to them.

Immigrants who arrive as small children or who are born to first-generation immigrant parents often grow up to do things their parents never imagined: They go to college and get jobs as doctors, engineers, lawyers, teachers, or business leaders, and they are able to give their children material things that they never had growing up.

What's more important to them, however, is for future generations to embrace their deep appreciation for the culture and values of their ancestors, as well as for the benefits of life in America. They know they've been given a gift. A gift of freedom. A gift of opportunity. And they typically feel a deep sense of gratitude and an obligation to share that gift with others.

Josephine Park, whose family emigrated from war-torn Vietnam when she was a child, has greatly benefited from those freedoms and opportunities. And she's discovered the joy that comes with pouring her experiences into the lives of others.

Josephine Park

Dr. Josephine Park no longer eats frogs,
but she'll never forget the impact they had on her journey.

The frog story always gets them.

Josephine Park tells it to her two children. She tells it when she speaks each year to a class of fourth graders at an elementary school in Fayetteville, Arkansas. She even tells it to some of her patients at her pediatric clinic. In fact, she tells it to just about anyone she thinks might learn something from her story.

Let's face it, when you tell people—especially kids—that your mother fed you frogs when you were a baby, it gets their attention. And if it doesn't, she can always tell them about sneaking out of Vietnam in the middle of the night. Or about being lost at sea for several days on a small fishing boat with no food or water.

But eating frogs is a good place to start, and not just because of its shock value. As it turns out, the frog story also has a prophetic edge to it, because Josephine Park, the former child refugee who once was healed by eating frogs in Vietnam, would become a pediatrician in America with a commitment to helping others, especially immigrants.

WHICH ONE IS BELLY?

On April 30, 1975, the North Vietnamese army entered Saigon, raised the Viet Cong flag, and effectively ended the country's long and brutal civil war.

Josephine was only 18 days old at the time. Her father had been a dentist, and her mother had run a coffee shop,

UNIVERSITY OF ARKANSAS
College of Arts & Sciences
May 10, 1997

but that was all before the communist takeover of South Vietnam. By the end of the war, the family had left all that they owned and moved to Binh Dinh, a small village along the country's south-central coast. Josephine's father spent three months in a "re-education camp" and then was given a plot of land to farm. It wasn't large enough to support his family, especially since a share of what he grew went to the government, and the family quickly felt the tightening grip of poverty.

When Josephine's sister was born in 1976, her mother stopped breastfeeding Josephine and instead gave that sustenance to the newborn. Josephine survived mostly on rice soup. By the time she was three, she was unable to walk. She had lost all of her hair, had rashes on much of her body, suffered from respiratory illnesses, and had a huge protuberant stomach.

"My nickname in my village was 'Belly' because that was the most noticeable part on me," she said.

With no access to medical care, the family turned to a Buddhist monk to break what they thought was a "spell" on their daughter. He performed some chants and prescribed a diet of frogs. They had magical powers that would break the spell, he told them.

"Frogs are not something you'd eat in Vietnam," Josephine said. "They're considered gross. So when Mother got those frogs, she would make them into eggrolls. My sisters would get so jealous, because eggrolls were a treat. She would pull them aside and say, 'These eggrolls are made of frogs.'"

After eating nearly 100 frogs, Josephine's physical condition improved. Her hair grew back. The rashes went away.

Her respiratory condition got better. And her belly slowly got smaller.

"I've never eaten frogs since those frogs," she said.

The frogs, of course, weren't filled with magic. They were filled with protein. Josephine was suffering from kwashiorkor, a form of severe malnutrition caused by protein deficiencies.

"My nickname, Belly, has stuck with me to this day," she said. "Every time I talk to relatives back in Vietnam, they don't know my name. They just know me as Belly. I put a photo on Facebook of me and my sisters. My cousin in Vietnam saw it, and he asked, 'Which one is Belly?'"

ESCAPING VIETNAM

By May 1979, just after her fourth birthday, the poverty and persecution had taken such a toll on Josephine's family that her parents decided to risk everything and flee. So in the middle of the night, they took their five daughters and left Vietnam.

"The only house we stopped at was my grandparents'," Josephine said. "That's my only memory. I don't remember the faces of my grandparents, but I remember being at their house and my parents saying we were leaving. I didn't know where we were leaving or where we were going."

The family boarded a fishing boat and left their homeland for a future that was totally undefined. The 90 other people crowded onto the boat included Josephine's uncle and his family of 12. They expected a four-day trip to "whatever country would accept us," but a storm took them off course, and they were in the open seas for seven days.

"We got lost, and we ran out of food and water," Josephine said. "I remember sitting in a boat and telling Mother I was really thirsty. I remember my younger sister...we both were asking for water. Mother said, 'Okay, I'll let you have a few drops. We just don't have much.'"

The boat eventually found its way to Hong Kong, where the family of seven shared a bunk bed in a refugee camp. Josephine remembers playing on the top bunk with her sisters and seeing other kids on the bunk next to them behind a blanket that served as a wall. She and her sisters spent their days in a red double-decker bus that was converted into a school for the refugee children, but about a year later the family was relocated to Fort Smith, Arkansas.

"It's amazing how we all made it out of Vietnam and survived," she said. "We always felt like God had a reason for our family to be here in America."

Josephine knew nothing about the United States when she arrived, however, and some of her first impressions weren't that good. In fact, she quickly formed a big misconception after seeing one of her first American movies—*Jaws*.

"I thought the whole country was surrounded by water and full of sharks," she said. "I had no idea how big America was. So that was my vision of America as a country. Lots of water and sharks."

Fort Smith turned out to be shark-free. It also already was home to a small but thriving Vietnamese community. Fort Chaffee, a nearby army training camp, had been used to house Vietnamese refugees from 1975-76. Many had stayed in the area because there were several factories that provided jobs that didn't require strong English-language skills. Eventually, some opened grocery stores, restaurants, or other businesses.

"Fort Smith was a great town," Josephine said. "The community was set up to help."

Grand Avenue Baptist Church, in particular, played a key role in her family's life. The church offered outreach services to the refugees, as well as a special worship service during which a translator would interpret for the pastor. Eventually, enough members of the Vietnamese community were attending that Grand Avenue helped them launch a church of their own with a pastor who spoke their native language.

For many immigrants who arrive as adults, the language barrier is one of the most difficult aspects of being in a new country. That was true for Josephine's parents.

"I remember taking them to the doctor and translating for them," she said. "I took them to the doctor instead of them taking me, which is so neat because I now have a lot of Hispanic families who come to our clinic, and their kids will translate for them. I see my family when I see them. It brings back so many memories. I love them, and I feel like I have a connection with them. I have my own scribe who helps me do my charts. I make sure my scribe is Spanish-speaking, so she can translate for me."

Josephine's mother had the equivalent of a fifth-grade education, and that would have been Josephine's fate had her family stayed in Vietnam. In America, however, she took full advantage of the educational opportunities. She graduated valedictorian of her high school in 1993, and that same year she and the rest of her family became naturalized U.S. citizens.

"We all took the test together and became American citizens at the same time," she said. "I remember proudly standing at the court house taking the Oath of Allegiance to the United States during our naturalization ceremony. We no longer had to use our 'Resident Alien' cards, and we were given the Certificates of Citizenship."

She then went to the University of Arkansas, where she graduated Summa Cum Laude from the Fulbright College honors program. During her junior year, she began dating Jong Sup Park, a Korean immigrant she had been friends with since high school. They married in 2000 and went to medical school together, with him focusing on radiology and her on pediatrics (Josephine's residency thesis was on child malnutrition).

In 2008, after a year in Connecticut where Jong had a fellowship with Yale University, they returned to Arkansas and began raising their family. They also began intentionally exploring how to fulfill a much deeper calling they felt in their lives.

LEAVING A LEGACY

When Josephine first arrived in America, her parents went to work at OK Foods, a factory that processed chickens. She and her sisters quickly picked up on their parents' sense of gratitude for the opportunities they were getting in their new country, so they all worked hard and did well in school. One of her sisters went on to become an electrical engineer, two became pharmacists, and another went into marketing. The fifth was unable to attend college because of an illness.

Their parents encouraged them to adapt to their new culture, but they also worked hard to ensure they remembered where they came from—the struggles, of course, but also the rich traditions of their Vietnamese culture and values.

For instance, they learned to respect and obey their parents and their teachers. In fact, Josephine always addresses her parents as Mother and Father, not him, she, her, he, or in any other less formal way. And at the dinner table, the children never began eating until their parents had begun.

They also spoke only Vietnamese in their home when they were growing up so that they would retain their native language. And their parents regularly told and retold stories about their life in Vietnam. To this day, Josephine doesn't specifically remember eating frogs, but her parents' stories provide her a memory that's just as real.

"They don't want us to forget our roots," she said. "They feel we'll never know how blessed we are if we don't remember where we came from. We came to America, and there was food. They would tell the stories over and over. They wanted us to do well, but they do not want us to forget where we are from."

Josephine and her husband want their children, Grace and Gideon, to appreciate their cultural roots and the values that they believe in. But it's been hard to teach them their languages. Josephine speaks English and some basic Vietnamese, while her husband speaks English and some basic Korean. Thus, they don't have conversations with each other in anything but English.

"We teach them some basic things so they can communicate with grandparents," Josephine said. "But we tell them a lot about where we're from. They will never experience some of the things my husband and I went through. They have a very blessed life. We've been able to provide material things, so they don't know what it's like not to have something. But we tell them my story. We tell them his story."

The Parks also are deeply involved in serving others, and not just through their medical practices.

"We often wondered why God would bring a little girl from a small village in Vietnam to Arkansas and a young boy from a small town in South Korea to Arkansas and allow them to meet, find God, and get married," Josephine said. "In 2008, we started having deep conversations about God's purpose for our lives and decided to start using the gifts and passions God has blessed us with to serve His kingdom."

They regularly go on medical mission trips to other countries, and they plan to take their children along as they get older "so they can see how blessed we are in this land."

They also are actively involved with international students who are attending the University of Arkansas. "Why not love on them?" Josephine said. "We were once one of them."

And they lead a study each summer on building healthier marriages. "We struggled so much our first few years," Josephine said. "So we invite co-workers, not just church members, and work with the people around us."

For Josephine and her husband, life has become about giving back—to their children, to their community, to their adopted country, and to the world.

"God has infused our lives with blessings ever since He allowed us to set foot upon this wonderful country," she said. "Our desire is to share the love and grace that God has generously blessed us with and to serve our Father until we see Him in our eternal Heaven. We always have our eyes and ears open for what God has in store next. We're still on our journey."

Olive Mbulambo

When Olive Mbulambo left the Congo, she had no idea that one day she would be fighting bullies and working to build the confidence of young women.

Born in the Congo at the close of the 20th century, Olive Mbulambo and her family learned early on how to pack up quickly and emigrate to another country. On the heels of the Rwandan genocide that triggered two consecutive wars in the Congo, Olive's father hastily moved the family to Cameroon, where he taught university courses in chemistry, math, and physics for nine years. During this time, he applied for refugee entrance into the United States. Olive's mother, a stay-at-home mom, was the steadying force that settled the family and made Cameroon home. "We never felt like a displaced people," recalled Olive. "My mom knows how to make a home."

Arriving home from school in 2009, Olive received the news that the family would be moving to America. They were joined by another African family and, with bags packed full of clothing, she endured several long plane flights to their destination: Boise, Idaho.

"I had never heard of Idaho," Olive laughed. "But we didn't care, as long as it was in America." She settled into an apartment with her four siblings, and quickly enrolled in school. Her father stressed the importance of education while he set about finding work to support his large family. He initially found work in the fields, picking peppers and onions throughout the winter. He then worked to get a Cer-

tified Nursing Assistant certification, and has been working in health care ever since.

"I learned hard work, dedication, and focus from my dad," recounted Olive. "His tireless work ethic and his refusal to complain, even when his hands were cracked and bleeding, has been a huge example to me." This example was pivotal when Olive entered Borah High School as a non-English speaking African in her sophomore year. "I not only had to learn, I had to learn in a completely foreign language," Olive recalls. "As an African, I definitely stood out, and was often bullied because I was different." She quickly learned that the manners common in Cameroon did not translate to the less formal attitude of American teenagers. "I guess in Cameroon, we found peace in our everyday lives by learning to respect those around us. Even if all of Africa was at war, we were taught peace in our homes and schools. And I was always taught that peace is better than war." Olive decided that bullying was a new kind of war, and instead of quitting, she set out to make sure she had an impact on kids by the time her siblings were in high school.

Her graduation from Borah High School was one of her proudest days. "I had crossed the Atlantic, learned a new language, mastered my classes, and made some friends. I stood there feeling like a girl who had defeated the odds." That summer, her father, who had by this time successfully gained citizenship for his family, enrolled Olive in the College of Western Idaho where she also became CNA-certified like her father. This inspired her transfer to Boise State University as a biology major, with the goal of someday traveling back to her native Africa to help young women in labor and delivery. "In Cameroon, if you had no money, you got no health care. I once witnessed a woman pregnant with twins die in childbirth, along with her babies, because she did not have enough money for help. In America, everyone gets health care and this doesn't happen," Olive recounted. "I want to teach women in Africa to help each other in childbirth, until the government follows countries like America and provides health care to all women."

While matriculating into Boise State University, Olive met another young student who had developed confidence, speaking skills, and connections through participation in pageants. This young woman encouraged Olive to consider joining a pageant to broaden her horizons. Finding very few national pageants available in Idaho, Olive applied to represent Idaho in the Miss USA Intercontinental pageant. After months of negotiating and gathering support, Olive was chosen as the first woman to represent Idaho in this pageant, where she won First Runner Up, Miss Congeniality, Best Interview, and Best Swimwear. Along the way, she overcame criticism by peers who told her that she would not make it, or succeed. These victories, and the focused work it took to get there, solidified in her mind that adolescents can overcome bullying, criticism, and discouragement by having mentors place the right ideas into their minds. "I had many teachers take the time and exhibit the patience necessary to teach me English and help me succeed in school. Whatever I do as a profession, I want to always be a mentor to young girls. I hope, along with my medical career, that I can be a pageant director someday, and instill young women with the confidence and positive ideas they need to flourish."

But first, Olive has one more year of rigorous coursework at Boise State. Her brother, a wrestler for the same university, is studying to be a doctor and keeps pushing her toward the finish line. Behind them both, every day, waits a stay-at-home-mom who has kept their feet grounded in their new home, and their eyes focused on their goals.

"Never underestimate the power of a stay-at-home-mom," Olive smiles broadly. "I have a lot of career goals, but really, I hope I have enough courage and strength to be like my mom. She is the one who took us from being foreigners in a new city, to citizens in a new home. Our home."

Barbaro Garbey

Barbaro Garbey left behind the world he knew in Cuba
for the chance to shine on the diamond in America.

In the late 1970s, Fidel Castro's government in Cuba was attempting to deal with a wave of discontent among citizens who wanted to leave the country to escape political oppression. At the same time, the U.S. government was seeking to improve its strained relationship with Castro.

As tensions rose on the island nation, thousands of people went to foreign embassies in search of sanctuary. Eventually, several nations, including the U.S., offered asylum to *bona fide* political prisoners. But the floodgates opened in April 1980, shortly after U.S. President Jimmy Carter announced America would accept up to 3,500 Cuban refugees. Castro then announced the port of Mariel would be open to anyone who wanted to go, and thousands upon thousands wanted to go.

The numbers quickly escalated. In all, around 125,000 Cubans came to America during a six-month stretch in 1980 in what became known as the Mariel boatlift, or the Freedom Flotilla.

Some left for political reasons. Some left for economic reasons. And some left because Castro didn't want them in Cuba. And so many of those contributed to the greater good of America by bringing blue-collar skills to the South Florida labor market. Some even would rise to fame, including painter and sculptor Carlos Alfonzo, opera singer Elizabeth Caballero, poet Reinaldo Arenas, Pulitzer Prize winner Mirta Ojito, and a hardscrabble baseball player named Barbaro

Garbey—the first Cuban from the Castro era to make it to the Major Leagues.

A BIG LEAGUE JOURNEY

Barbaro Garbey chuckled at the idea that long bus rides are some sort of inconvenience in life.

"You are talking with a Cuban who came on a boat for 12 hours," he said. "No pressure for me to be on a bus for six or seven hours."

In 2016, the 59-year-old Barbaro finished his fifth year as a coach with the Mississippi Braves, a Class AA minor league baseball team. Long bus rides were the norm. When the season ended, he headed to Venezuela to coach in a winter league with more bus rides.

That's his life. A good life.

"I'm just happy to stay in baseball," he said. "It doesn't matter what level. As long as I can continue to teach and stay in baseball, I'm happy. This is the game I love. That's the only thing I know. So I'm very satisfied."

To the young athletes he now mentors and coaches, Barbaro offers much more than help with baseball skills. They might, at first, see him as just another guy who has spent a lifetime bouncing around professional baseball with an all-too-brief taste of the Big Leagues. When they get to know him, however, they find that his personal journey represents the power of persistence, the value of second chances, and the importance of following your passions in life.

For Barbaro, that passion has always been baseball. It's a game he loves so much, in fact, that he walked away from everything he knew in Cuba—and everyone he knew, as well—on the belief that he could make it to the Major

Leagues as a player. And he did. But like so many parts of his journey, it seldom came easily, and never without a price.

FROM STAR TO REFUGEE

Barbaro came from an athletic family and was identified early on as a baseball talent. He was the youngest of nine siblings who included a brother who was champion boxer and a sister who was a star track athlete. His brother, in fact, won a gold medal as a light-middleweight in the 1967 Pan American Games, a silver in the 1968 Olympics, and a bronze in the 1976 Olympics. And his sister finished fourth in the long jump at the 1972 Olympics.

So it was no surprise when Barbaro, at age 11, was sent to the Sport Initiation School in Havana to be groomed for a career as a baseball player.

"My life in Cuba was not bad at all," Barbaro said. "From the time I was 11 or 12, we'd go to school in the morning, practice in the afternoon, go to bed, and go home on weekends. So I was well-prepared. I started playing at the elite level in Cuba."

He was only 17 in 1974 when he debuted on the Cuban national team, and he quickly became a celebrity in the baseball-crazed nation. But he was earning only 95 pesos a month—about $860 a year—and in 1978 he was caught taking money on the side from gamblers to shave runs and keep games close. Just like that, Barbaro was out of baseball.

He needed a way to provide for his wife and two young daughters, and he longed to prove himself as one of the best of the best in baseball. He might have stayed and worked his way back onto the national team, but the Mariel boatlift in 1980 provided another opportunity—the chance to play professionally in America.

Fidel Castro had agreed to let anyone leave who wanted to go, but there were no guarantees that the promise would apply to Barbaro. Under Castro, no Cuban-born player had ever gone to America and made it to the Major Leagues. There were no guarantees that Barbaro would make a team if he made it to America, or that he would even get the chance to try out. So with all of those unknowns, Barbaro and his wife decided she should stay behind with their children.

"We decided to do it that way because I didn't know what to expect when I came over here," he said. "I didn't want to bring the family and start a new life without knowing. I wanted to get on my feet and bring them over later."

It would be a risk, to be sure. But it was a risk he believed was worth taking—if only he could get off the island. Even though he no longer was a member of the national team, he was still a well-known baseball player from a family of talented athletes. He wasn't someone the Castro government wanted to put on the boats that were shuttling people to America. So he had to work the system just to get a ticket.

"I had to go to the immigration office about three times," he said. "They told me the situation was not for me. A lot of people who were going had been in jail or the government wanted to get them out of the country for some other reason. So I persevered."

Eventually, Barbaro traded his documents with someone who had a criminal background, and he was given the necessary papers to leave the country. "That's how I got through," he said. "Even then, some officials recognized me and put pressure on me not to leave."

For Barbaro, however, there was no turning back. He joined another 200 refugees on a boat, and they hunkered down for the journey into the unknown. The capacity for the craft was only 80 people, so it was jam-packed. And a brutal storm blew in, making the trip more miserable. The 90-mile crossing to Key West, Florida, took 12 hours, but each minute brought them closer and closer to something they didn't have in Cuba—hope.

"It was a long boat ride," Barbaro said, "but no one was thinking about the long boat ride. They were thinking about getting to America and starting a new life."

STARTING OVER

Barbaro, like the others on the trip, arrived with nothing but the clothes he was wearing. The refugees were transported three hours north, checked into a camp in Miami, fed, and given a couple of t-shirts and a place to sleep.

Most were moved to other camps around the country, until they were released into the care of a relative—if a relative could find them. Barbaro was sent to Fort Indiantown, Pennsylvania, where he and the other refugees spent their days playing cards or street baseball as they waited for the future to unfold.

"It wasn't like a prison," he said, "but there was not freedom there."

Orlando Pena, a Cuban-born scout with the Detroit Tigers who had pitched in the Big Leagues, spotted Barbaro's name among the refugee list published in the *Miami Herald*. He tracked Barbaro down, but Barbaro hardly resembled the muscular star who had shown so much promise in Cuba.

"When he showed up in the camp, we had been in there for about a month," said Barbaro, who was wearing rolled up jeans and a t-shirt the day Pena found him playing pepper at the refugee camp. "We were not looking good there. I had the same pair of pants. I was losing weight. I was worrying about what the situation would be. It was not a good situation."

Pena introduced himself, and Barbaro made him a promise: Feed me well, give me a chance, and I'll show you I can still hit.

Pena offered him $2,500 to sign with the Tigers, which, of course, Barbaro readily accepted. A few weeks later, a cousin who also had spotted his name in the *Miami Herald* drove to Pennsylvania, and took Barbaro to her home in New York. Then he flew to Florida to join the Tigers' Class A team in Lakeland.

CURVEBALLS AND SLIDERS

Barbaro's rise through the minors was relatively quick but often tumultuous. He excelled in the outfield, where he played when he wasn't the designated hitter. But he spoke no English, which made it hard to communicate with his coaches, bond with teammates, or to even order a meal. While he was in Lakeland, he had a teammate who could translate, but he was the only Latino on the team when he advanced to Double-A.

"I was willing to do whatever I could to make it to the Major Leagues," he said. "That's the only way I could help my family back in Cuba. I was not making that much, but I tried to help them as much as I could. It took a long time to adjust. After the season, I was living in Miami. I was around some cousins, and that made it a little easier. But I was missing family more. Miami was like Cuba but without my family. I did not feel comfortable. America wasn't my home."

There was no going back, and it soon became clear that his family wasn't going to join him in America. As he struggled to adapt to a new culture, he and his wife divorced.

"My family was supposed to come after me," he said. "Then my wife's mother got sick. Then her older sister died. It was difficult for her to leave her family there, so they decided not to come because of the situation in Cuba. So I decided to continue with my life."

Some of his troubles in Cuba also followed him to the United States. In May 1983, while he was in the process of hitting .321 for the Tigers' Triple-A team in Evansville, Indiana, a story broke about his involvement in the run-shaving scandal. A few fans harassed him relentlessly about it during games, and one incident led to an off-the-field altercation after a game. Words were exchanged and Barbaro hit the heckler across the shoulder with a fungo bat. He felt certain his baseball career had just ended.

Charges were filed but were later dropped; still, Barbaro was suspended from the team for 30 days. Had it not been for the incident and the suspension, Barbaro likely would have been promoted to Detroit that year. Instead, he waited and made the team's opening-day roster in 1984.

"Making it to the Major Leagues was my goal, and I felt satisfied," he said. "I did not leave Cuba in vain."

Barbaro became a valuable contributor to one of the best teams in Detroit's history, playing for future Hall of Fame manager, Sparky Anderson, and alongside stars like Lance Parrish, Dave Bergman, Lou Whitaker, Alan Tram-

mell, Darrell Evans, Kirk Gibson, and Jack Morris. He hit
.287 in 110 games during the regular season, and the Tigers
went on to beat San Diego in the World Series.

"I was happy to be the first Cuban from the Castro era
to play in the Major Leagues," he said. "I had the satisfac-
tion to play for that great team in 1984—all those great
teammates. I really appreciated it. We won the World Series.
That was the highlight of my career."

Barbaro played the next season with the Tigers, who finished third in their division. He hit .257 in 86 games, and
played sparingly at the end of the year as the team focused
on younger players. He was traded to Oakland in the off
season, but was released by the A's in March of 1985.

After that, Barbaro bounced around in professional
baseball, mostly playing in the Mexican League, although
he made a brief comeback with the Texas Rangers in 1987.
Age and injuries were catching up to him, however, and he
never made it back to the Big Leagues after that. He spent
another six seasons in the minors or playing in Mexico, before retiring as a player. Most of his career since then has
been as a coach in the minor leagues.

GROWING UP

Looking back, Barbaro recognizes that one of the things
that held him back was immaturity on and off the field. He
didn't always handle "freedom" well, he said, and at times
took it for granted. And as a player, he said he didn't fully
understand what it took to be a true professional.

"When I was playing with the Tigers, I was a rookie in
every sense of the word," he said. "I had the same discipline
I had in Cuba, which was not that much. Over here, you

have to learn how to be a good teammate, how to follow the rules, how to settle down and be a professional. I learned how to be a professional really when I was in Mexico. I played there seven years. I learned how you act, how you treat teammates, what teammates expect from you."

Now, the minor leagues are filled with Latino players and Barbaro tries to share lessons of life with them, as well lessons about hitting a baseball.

"It's more satisfying to me just to continue to teach the young kids, the American kids and the Latinos, to show them the way to make it to the higher level," he said. "Based on my experience, I can contribute advice they need. They have a lot more opportunity than I had when I came. They should take advantage of it."

Because he moved around so much, Barbaro never applied for citizenship. But in 1985, his second season with the Tigers, he remarried and started a second family in America. He and his wife, Kimberly, have a home outside of Detroit in Livonia, Michigan, where they have raised three children.

He's also been able to see his Cuban family. When he was playing in Mexico, his mother traveled there and he spent time with her. She passed away a year later, so he was thankful that he saw her that final time. One of his older daughters from his first marriage now lives in Las Vegas, so he's able to stay in touch with her. And in December 2015, with relationships improved between Cuba and America, he returned to Havana for the first time since leaving, staying for a week and seeing family there.

"Everyone was happy to see me," he said, "and I was happy to see them. They treated me fine."

After more than 35 years in America, Barbaro feels at home in his adopted country and thankful for the life he's lived and that he's living.

"I really appreciate being here in America," he said. "I grew up. I learned the culture. I don't think I could live anywhere else. Everywhere I worked, everywhere I played, people treated me very well. I really appreciate it. I consider America to be my country. I have spent more time in the U.S. than in Cuba. I have my family and my friends. Life here for me is very, very good."

FINAL THOUGHTS

By Mark Russell

Refugees are a unique subset of immigrants. A uniqueness implied by the term refugee; they are a group of people seeking safety or refuge. Unlike a lot of immigrants who consciously choose to move and intentionally select the United States as their destination, refugees are forced out of their homeland and generally come to the U.S. because of international agreements.

Receiving people from troubled parts of the world who are not always in great condition is frequently met with a range of confusion and steadfast resistance. One of the fundamental questions we face is: Is America better with or without this immigrant? In terms of refugees, we could rephrase and ask: Does it benefit America to have refugees?

An underlying premise to this question is also, *What is the right thing to do*? Our history has shown us that when we do the right thing in the long term, over a broad range of people, then it will benefit us.

On what basis and how many refugees we accept is a complex and situational question that is outside of the scope of this book. But I would like to outline a few reasons why I do believe it benefits America to be a leading nation in accepting refugees.

1) To build our compassion and adjust our perspective

Most refugees are fleeing situations that are way beyond the experiences of native-born Americans; some are borderline unbelievable. We will be featuring many of them throughout our series.

Getting to know them and their stories puts our own challenges in perspective. Undoubtedly, many native-born Americans do face significant challenges in life. But many complaints belong in the "first-world problems" category of challenges. In other words, they pale in comparison to what refugees have, in general, gone through.

Allowing refugees helps us to know them and their stories, and helps us become more compassionate people with a better perspective on the world.

2) To relieve pressures on Europe

Currently, there is massive migration going on in Europe. Pressure is mounting. Race-based exclusion, once hush-hush in the wake of the Nazi disaster, is rising again. It is becoming increasingly more acceptable to focus on unique people groups and intentionally isolate and exclude them.

This is not helping the European cause at all. This exclusionary focus breeds contempt. We have seen tensions flaring over the past year.

If the migration continues unabated and the pushback against it intensifies, which it almost certainly will, we could be facing a very serious situation. While the U.S. and no single country could take the influx of refugees, anything we do to relocate and help these refugees will translate to relieving pressure in Europe, which in the long run will be really good for us all, Americans, Europeans and refugees alike.

3) To serve as a model for other countries

As my co-author, Dick Gephardt, frequently points out, no other nation has done immigration the way we have. It is how this nation was formed, and it is something we have done, albeit not always perfectly, but continually throughout our history.

By continuing to accept refugees and helping them transition, we continue to serve as a model to the rest of the world on how it can be done well. It's a model the world desperately needs. We are an increasingly interconnected world, and we are not isolated from conflicts around the world. We can't ignore these countries' conflicts. Their conflicts will become our conflicts.

Serving as a model empowers other countries to also accept refugees and thereby diminish tension around the world.

4) To diminish the power of the terrorist

Refugees, by definition, are fleeing danger or some sort of persecution. While this can be drought or natural disaster-induced, it is frequently because of violence. They have an enemy who is trying to do them in.

There are many problems with trying to prevent a particular type of refugee—a Muslim, for example— from entering our country, but one of the main problems is that exclusion empowers the rhetoric and the position of the ones who thrive on violence.

Many Muslims, for example, are being persecuted and are fleeing that persecution. By inviting them into our country, we show them that we care about them, which inevitably diminishes the power of the violent-prone, anti-American people behind the persecution. If we close our borders to any people group, we give evidence to the violent-prone, Anti-Americans that we are as bad as they say we are. This makes their job of recruitment and radicalization much easier.

It is actually strategic to accept as many people as we can from the parts of the world, where there are strongholds of people who are working against us. Initially, this seems counterintuitive, but with some reflection, its validity becomes clear. The more people whom we welcome and care for, the more people who have an understanding of who Americans really are.

THE POOR

INTRODUCTION

By Dick Gephardt

America is a big country. That's not an earth-shattering revelation, of course. But it's not just big geographically speaking—although, at more than 3.8 million square miles, it leaves a hefty footprint.

The vastness of its area contributes to its diversity and makes it, as a country, big in many other ways. Big opportunities. Big challenges. Big complexities. Big ideas. Big dreams. Big, big, big. And for many newcomers, all that bigness can feel overwhelming. On a map, in books, and even in movies and television, America often is presented in digestible slices. In person, it can be a lot to swallow.

Nabiel Fareed was one of those immigrants who arrived with big ambitions and a big belief in what America could offer, but very little in the way of a specific plan for making those dreams come true or how to face the big challenges that inevitably came his way.

Like many other newcomers, he simply went to work and made life happen, never giving up and never giving in. And along the way, he has lived a big life and is leaving a big legacy in his big adopted country.

Nabiel Fareed

Nabiel Fareed's leap of faith—that God's will be done—took him across the Atlantic for an unimaginable journey.

The agent for Trans World Airlines at John F. Kennedy Airport in New York grew frustrated. She didn't know how to help the passenger, and he wasn't going away. Other passengers, meanwhile, stood in line waiting.

And waiting.

And waiting.

Nabiel Fareed did his best to restate his need, but broken English, fatigue, and a few muddled-up facts all conspired against him.

"I am going to Oklahoma State University," Nabiel said again, "in Salt Lake City, Utah."

The agent sighed.

"That cannot be," she said again.

Finally, she asked him to step aside and wait for a supervisor so she could help the other customers.

"I did not understand fully what she said," Nabiel said as he recalled that day in 1968, "but tears filled my eyes and it hit me so hard: I am alone and know no one here I can call for help."

He had traveled from his home in the Palestinian village of Kufr Rai', boarded an airplane in Amman, Jordan, and, after a long layover in Madrid, Spain, he had finally reached New York. Now he had $965 in his pocket and a single goal: make his way to Oklahoma State University in Salt Lake City, Utah and figure out how to enroll in college.

"I didn't have any clue," he said. "I didn't have a scholarship. I didn't know exactly what I needed. I just needed to get there and from there I would have to deal with things and accept whatever was needed to reach my goal, which was to get an education."

Now that plan had hit a significant snag.

In that crushing moment of fear and despair, a man in the line stepped forward to help.

"He had heard the repeated loud exchange and noticed my confusion, despair, sadness, and helplessness," Nabiel said. "He smiled at me first, then identified himself to the agent and told her to book me to Tulsa, Oklahoma and that he would take care of me."

This was the America that Nabiel had heard about and dreamed of while growing up.

"I came to America in search of a way to change my life, but I didn't know how I could do this and how I could survive knowing no one to ask for support, help, or guidance," he said. "And that really scared me and ate on me a lot. The minute I arrived, I was greeted with the humanity I had heard so much about but had never witnessed before…God sent me immediate help at the TWA arrival desk that day."

That humanity came in the form of James Whatley, the Dean of the College of Agriculture at Oklahoma State University. He was returning from a conference when he overheard Nabiel's dilemma and provided assistance. Whatley flew with Nabiel to Tulsa, drove him the two hours to the OSU campus in Stillwater, Oklahoma, put him in a dorm room, and told him how to register for classes the next day. When Nabiel looked confused, the professor made it simple.

"He grabbed a piece of paper and wrote down, 'Registrar's Office, 8 a.m.,'" Nabiel recalled.

So on the last day of registration, Nabiel began an academic career that would prove foundational to his new life in America—a life that included a successful career in international business and produced four children who have gone on to highly successful careers of their own.

"The Dean, may God bless his soul, not only gave me an anchor, but he really gave me a lifeline," said Nabiel. "I owed him so much gratitude I cannot describe in words."

On the morning he went to register for classes, Nabiel noticed a poster on a wall in the dormitory where he was staying. It said, "Some people are told, 'You can't do that,' and it crushes them. Other people say, 'I'll show you.'"

It was as if the message had been posted just for him.

He read it every day for weeks and eventually wrote it down.

"It became my roadmap," he said. "It became very clear to me that the opportunity to achieve and improve ourselves is not predetermined at birth; that upward mobility, while hard, is possible. Every dream comes with a price tag. You must earn it. So to make my dreams come true, I must embrace the work and take action. I must study hard and not squander opportunities. I kept telling myself that the worst enemy to success is self-doubt and that hard work can lead to bigger and better changes."

UP FROM THE OLIVE GROVES

As a child, Nabiel had a favorite toy: the world map.

"I'd look at it, read it, stare at it, and then dream of this different U.S.A. place," he said. "Peace-loving people with so many amazing opportunities."

A very different place from what he saw all around him.

Nabiel's father was a member of an elite army/police unit in Jaffa that was formed by the British Mandate of Palestine, but he and his family moved with the creation of the state of Israel. They settled in Kufr Rai', a rural village about 100 kilometers (62 miles) northwest of Tel Aviv. His father carried on the family business of growing and selling olive products. They were respected members of the community, but it was a community in constant strife.

Born in 1944, he was the oldest son in a family with 10 children. Two of his sisters—one younger than him and the other older—died young from the measles. Nabiel and his other siblings were raised with no electricity and no running water in a two-story, six-room house his father built amidst the olive trees on the five acres the family owned.

"I was brought up with very little money," he said. "In reality, there was little need for money. There was not much to buy. I was told not to strive for money or success, as that may lead me to end up greedy or big-headed, which only leads to unhappiness."

Nabiel learned about life and work from his father and grandfather, from their stories as well as from their examples. They taught him how to plant crops, build a fire, speak bluntly but respectfully, solve problems, and share wisdom through stories.

"There were more opportunities for different generations to interact," he said. "Their joys and sorrows served as examples for us to learn from, to emulate, or, perhaps even more useful, to avoid."

His family set high expectations of him, and at an early age he became determined to build a better life. He saw a region ravaged by war and refugee families with children who were hungry, homeless, and hopeless. He wanted something better for his children.

In the midst of this, he met a teacher who had studied in the United States. He was different. He dressed different. He acted different. He taught different. He told Nabiel how he had studied in the U.S.A., "in Utah," and that OSU also was a good college. That became Nabiel's goal.

"Early in life, I was forced to understand the importance of taking responsibility," he said. "That helped me create a reservoir of good feelings that I tapped into when things got hard. I was willing to risk change and accept the challenge of working toward the realization of my dreams, as well as improving the quality of life for my family.

"My goal was to figure out what my family needs and what I must do to help. Bring my family across a bridge or build a bridge that my family can cross to a new life away from war and destruction? The one thing I knew with complete clarity was that I wanted to uplift myself and my family to a better life and better opportunities."

Nabiel was 24 when he arrived in America. He worked his way through Oklahoma State, earning both a Bachelor's Degree and a Master's Degree, then earned a Doctorate in International Relations and Public Administration at Washington State.

One summer, his family introduced him to Wesam, the 17-year-old daughter of a respected mason. With blessings from both families, a year-long courtship began between Wesam, who was living in the West Bank town of Nablus, and Nabiel, who was in America. The letters written during this period became famous within the family for their sincerity, the dreams they shared, and, most of all, for the depiction of America that Nabiel provided to his future wife.

When they finally began their life together in America, they did so on a foundation of belief, not guarantees—two young, wide-eyed immigrants trying to make their marriage into a family in America. Nabiel became a top student in his Ph.D. program. To help make ends meet, he moonlighted as a bus driver, worked in a local church, was a teaching assistant, and served as a translator.

Wesam supported him and their family along their journey. When the studio apartment they lived in would get too cold in winter or when they needed more milk and had no way to buy it, Wesam always found a way. In love and with a commitment to their mutual growth together, they did everything as a team.

When he no longer qualified for a school visa, Nabiel traveled back-and-forth to America on business until gaining U.S. citizenship in 1984.

"The oil boom of 1977 brought unprecedented business opportunities for American companies to do business in the Middle East," he said. "But there was a huge shortage of educated, bilingual Arab-Americans. I got involved in this first as a part-time consultant for a large company in Tulsa."

Later, Nabiel opened a company in New York that exported and shipped American medical supplies to Saudi Arabia and the Gulf states. After the Oslo Peace Accord was signed in 1993 between Israel and the Palestine Liberation Organization (PLO), Nabiel helped start and lead the Palestinian American Chamber of Commerce as a step to "promote peace through business." The group had an office in New York and worked in cooperation with Israel until renewed hostilities between Israel and the PLO caused the PACC to shut down.

"We tried!" Nabiel said.

He and Wesam had four children, all born in the United States: Cynthia Hazar Fareed, an international lawyer in New York; Dr. Fareed Fareed, a graduate of Harvard Medical School and award-winning emergency room physician in New York; Emad Fareed, a partner at the international audit company, KPMG; and Morad Fareed, a successful entrepreneur whose credits include Delos Living and Square Roots.

"First and foremost, you start to understand what the word *risk* actually means and how we misunderstand it," Morad said when reflecting on the impact of his father's journey. "I can risk nothing. The immigrant risks everything. My only response to the blessings of being a first-generation American is relentless work. Though, to be honest, it's not optional or conscious. It's in my nature, and I'm sure in others like me, to make as much of ourselves as we can, and that means fire—the passion to never give up on the things you find important."

SHAPING THE FUTURE

When he was only two, Nabiel knocked over a gasoline lamp in a stairwell at his grandmother's house and suffered burns on the side of his head. The nurse at the local clinic said nothing could be done other than to pray *inshallah*—God's will be done.

It's a common expression among people of all different faiths in the Arabic-speaking world, and one that Nabiel and his family used (and still use) often. But with her son's life in peril, Nabiel's desperate mother wanted to make sure she did her part, as well. Her husband was away on business in Jaffa, an area within Tel Aviv. So she drove Nabiel two hours to Jaffa to a hospital that was staffed by British and American volunteers.

A recently arrived American physician had experience with burn injuries and turned out to be the answer to the family's prayers. Nabiel stayed in the hospital for two months, but eventually recovered.

Nabiel has tried several times over the years to track down the physician, known to him only as "Dr. George." But he's never been able to meet and thank the man he credits with saving his life. He takes comfort and pride, however, in the fact that one of his sons, Fareed Fareed, became a doctor.

The day his son decided to make emergency medicine his specialty was one of the best days of Nabiel's life.

"I was so thrilled and happy that I cried with joy, telling myself that although I failed to find Dr. George, my son is now a specialist who will save lives and carry that legacy with pride and honor," he said.

The success of his children is a great source of pride for Nabiel. It was for their future that he came to America. But their success, he said, would be incomplete if they failed to take away the lessons handed down from generation to generation in their family—lessons he learned at the feet of his parents and grandparents, aunts and uncles. And lessons he learned as he found his way in America.

"The most intriguing thing I found was the triumph and adaptability of the human spirit," he said. "The more challenges I faced, the more I simply adapted to them. I told myself that all problems, trials, and challenges that I will face are gifts given to learn, to help me grow, and prepare for things that I have the potential to do and become more successful."

He tried to teach his children to ignore skeptics but to learn from criticism, to take risks with their curiosity, to value family as a key to happiness, and to embrace the power of optimism.

"Those who have an optimism about what can be done will shape the future," he said.

He wanted his children to have the best of both worlds: The benefits of America and the strong cultural roots and traditions from their Palestinian heritage. So he took them to his homeland so they could not only hear stories about his life there, but see what it was like and learn from the family who still lived there.

"Every summer growing up, our parents would take us for summer break to Palestine," said Morad. "It was heaven. There was always energy and something happening: eat, play, laugh, games, huge afternoons with huge families! I didn't want to leave that Palestine. When we stopped these trips, I was 13 and I was old enough to understand what war meant. But I wondered how hard it must be not to be able to go back somewhere and only exist to go forward. That's the character of an immigrant."

Morad, who graduated from New York University as a decorated All-American scholar athlete, said his life was shaped constantly by his parents' ingenuity and energy. That's what inspired him to leave his business career in New York for two years so he could try out for and help form the ragtag first Palestine National Soccer team. The film, *Goal Dreams,* captured the team's historic journey to compete in the 2006 World Cup and allowed Morad to travel back to

Palestine again. The experience allowed him to live out the values he learned from his immigrant parents.

"It's not just work ethic," he said. "The work is secondary. We always must do something. That's all. Even if you're a child. Build something. Stare at the diplomas on the wall and create something. It's beyond determination. It's focus and fire. From a young age, I got to see a lot of different models of how things really happen. Creating is what the first generation is really blessed with."

The most poignant connection for Morad between his personal opportunities for success in America and his father's sacrifices and roots came during one of those summer trips to Palestine.

He was five years old, and they were staying in his dad's childhood home in Kufr Rai'. While playing outside with his brother, Morad felt a sharp pain on his thumb from the sting of a scorpion. His grandmother heard his screams and came running. She killed the scorpion, then rubbed a leaf on the bite while waiting on her husband to bring the car so they could take Morad to the hospital.

When they returned home a few hours later, his grandparents made him feel special by giving him some new toys and making him a bed to lay on in their living room. That's when he first noticed something that had been there all along.

Looking up from the floor, his eyes were drawn to a framed photo hanging on the wall. There were no other photos on this wall. Just this one. It was a picture of his father, Nabiel Fareed. Graduating.

Morris Drachman

*Morris Drachman found his treasure in an unlikely place—
in the discarded debris of New York City.*

*I sat there sobbing my eyes out. I'm not sure why, but the sheer
courage of a 27-year-old, leaving his wife, children, and all
he knew for a country that was only a vague mystical promise
of a future is just mind-boggling to me. I can only liken it to
signing up to be the first colonist to Mars today, only I would
have a better idea of what was in store for me.*

-Jay Baitler

As retired American executive, Jay Baitler, stepped foot on
Ellis Island, he did not linger with most of the solemn visi-
tors. The rational calculations of a businessman were unchar-
acteristically swept to the Hall of Records by what he can
only claim were the "spirits that inhabit the place." Circum-
venting the tour, he found a computer and within minutes
was staring at the record of his grandfather's crossing: *Morris
Drachman, 27-years-old, Married, Leather Worker, February
13, 1904, SS New York from Southampton.* The page blurred
and without warning, a flash flood of tears engulfed him as
he beheld the evidence of sheer courage. There was just no
calculating how a man at that age could leave a wife and
three toddlers, for the unknown land across the Atlantic.

A leather worker by trade, Morris Drachman arrived
in New York and immediately set out looking for work,
trudging the streets with the other immigrants. His head
held high, he beheld his new surroundings with a withering

stare full of understanding, courage, and a few secrets. His gait hinted at a limp. Wounded in the leg during one of the Jewish pogroms that stretched from Warsaw to Russia at the turn of the century, this leg would be lost entirely in his advanced years. This same leg held him steady as he finally found work driving a junk wagon, picking up debris throughout New York City.

It was the threat of war, and the foresight that there would not be any place for the Jews, that drove Morris to step onto the SS New York in 1904. He didn't need a fiddler on the roof to tell him that being drafted into the Polish army was a death sentence. His experience in that pogrom also sealed the certainty that to be a Jewish civilian may be a slower death sentence, but a death sentence it would be. He promised his wife that once he had made enough money and found accomodations, she and the children would follow.

For an entire year, Morris worked tirelessly, picking up trash, construction waste, city waste; anything discarded went into his wagon. He criss-crossed the city from one end to the other—over and over—until he became more intimately familiar with the sights, sounds, and goings-on of each city block, than a 20th-century town car driving Giuliani. He not only learned to command the landscape of New York, Morris was able to save enough money to bring his wife and three children, ages four, two and one, to join him. Esther Malke Drachman, age 25, gathered up the family and set sail for America just one year later. Little did Morris know, his wife would also find a way to smuggle her mother onboard at the last minute. He was surprised when five family members, instead of four, disembarked in New York.

A leatherworker, Morris was no stranger to the accumulaton of debris as he worked to cut, emboss, condition, and fasten rivets into the hides he worked in his youth. He also had learned the enormous value of recycling the debris left behind each project. It was with this mind of an artisan and the courage of an immigrant, that he eventually started his own demolition business. He had watched every builiding go up in New York City, and he became the expert on just how to take each building down. Knowing the difference between debris and salvage was his brilliance, and as he was hired to demolish everything from the Polo Grounds to the Ritz and Vanderbilt Hotels, not one brass knob or piece of scrap metal was sent to the landfill. It was not long before Morris Drachman was the go-to guy for demolition, and his mastermind of detail became the gift he passed on to his own sons, who carried on the business for decades. Through the business of demolition, Morris built a successful life for his family, earned the respect of the New York business community, and showed his children how to recognize that there is value in wreckage.

Wiping his tears and leaving the spirits that pulled him into the records hall on Ellis Island, Jay Baitler sat at his own computer and paid homage to his legacy with a beautiful post on Facebook about the courage of his 27-year-old grandfather. For the grandfather who had to tear down his whole life in Poland, the value of the life he salvaged and rebuilt in America, which continues to profit Jay, his own wife who immigrated to be his bride, and his grandchildren who now know a lot more about where they came from and how refuse can be one of life's greatest treasures.

FINAL THOUGHTS

By Mark Russell

"Give me your tired, your poor, your huddled masses yearning to breathe free," so says the most famous line inscripted on the Statue of Liberty. From the beginning and throughout history, the United States has been very egalitarian in immigration, in the sense that our immigration has not been based on already-acquired status and privilege but the human right for freedom and opportunity. We believe that is the right way to be. And our operating assumption is that if it's the right way, then there are benefits to it, especially in the long term.

As Dick pointed out earlier, drive and gratitude deeply define the poor who come to this country. The power of this is that the poor who have no drive do not get up and move across land and sea to a foreign country. By definition, the immigrants who arrive here are the motivated, get-things-done subset of people around the world. And because of that, they are able to take advantage of the opportunities in the United States and we are able to benefit from their hard work in numerous ways.

In addition to their drive and gratitude, a large percentage of these immigrants are taking the long view on their transition and are really looking to position their children in an environment more conducive to their well-being.

Both of our stories, Nabiel Fareed and Morris Drachman, illustrate the generational effect that those escaping poverty have. Their children and grandchildren and great grandchildren are much better off than they would have been. But is America better off? Obviously, yes. We have benefited from the generations of immigrants whose parents may have benefited from the move, but the children and subsequent generations benefited and contributed so much more.

Great nations are not built overnight, but over generations. America's benevolent approach to accepting the poor is not only right, but also a shrewd move that has enabled us to get the most driven people from around the world, who have helped build our great nation, and whose children have continued to make us great generation after generation.

THE MUSLIM

INTRODUCTION

By Dick Gephardt

When General William Sherman addressed the graduating class of the Michigan Military Academy in June 1879, he knew they felt a natural desire to take the skills they had learned and use them in a real war.

"Suppress it!" he told them. "You don't know the horrible aspects of war. I've been through two wars and I know. I've seen cities and homes in ashes. I've seen thousands of men lying on the ground, their dead faces looking up at the skies. I tell you, war is hell!"

Indeed, he knew. Sherman is perhaps most famous for his "March to the Sea" that wiped out much of Georgia's infrastructure during America's Civil War.

Aside from the attack on Pearl Harbor in 1941, America has avoided significant military campaigns within its borders since the war between her States. The rest of the world hasn't been so fortunate. And the fallout, to paraphrase Sherman, has been hell, especially on those who aren't part of the conflict, but who are swept into it by circumstances.

Many see family member killed or forced into the battles around them. Amid the destruction, they lose their homes and their sense of safety. So men, women, and children leave, all looking for hope in a new country.

They bring with them heartbreaking stories of their past, but their challenges seldom end when they arrive. Life in America is different. Better, yes. But not always easy. It might not be the hell they left behind, but it's not quite heaven, either. With courage and the help of family and new friends, however, these refugee immigrants often thrive and become new threads of fabric in the American tapestry.

Asmaa Albukaie

*Asmaa Albukaie took an unexpected path
to an unexpected place: Idaho.*

Asmaa Albukaie was a little girl growing up in Damascus, Syria when her grandmother told her where babies come from. There were no storks involved in this version. There were no birds or bees, either. Just beans.

You put some beans in your hand, her grandmother told her, and in the morning…babies!

It's easy to imagine a wide-eyed Asmaa looking up at her smiling grandmother, one wondering if this could possibly be true and the other wondering if her innocent little granddaughter was buying it.

In time, of course, Asmaa learned a more biologically accurate version. She was married at 14—not uncommon for girls in her culture—and she had two children of her own by the time she was 16—all without the help of storks, birds, bees, or beans.

Asmaa likes to tell the story about her grandmother now because it drives home a particularly relevant point in her life story: Not everything you hear is true.

As a single mother, a Syrian refugee, and a Muslim living in Boise, Idaho, Asmaa needs an oversized purse to carry all the stereotypes people might use to label her. But many of those stereotypes are like her grandmother's story of the beans, and she's determined to face them and defeat them with the most powerful weapon on earth: love.

Thankfully, that's one thing she brought with her from Damascus.

PREPARING FOR AN UNKNOWN JOURNEY

The preparation for Asmaa's journey to America began long before she had any idea it would ever take place.

First, there was the perspective she would have on life that came from her immediate family. In a country filled with religious diversity and division, her father preached love rather than hate. She was taught to share what she had—everything from food to friendship—with others, regardless of their beliefs. While this might not be part of the Islam many Americans have heard of, it was the Islam of her father.

Second, there was the perspective she would have on America that came from the movies. As a girl, Asmaa would hide in the family bathroom and watch American films on her laptop computer, then practice speaking English in the mirror. She had no plans to visit the United States, much less move here. She just liked to learn.

The movies gave her something more than rudimentary language lessons. Films like *Titanic* had heroines with strong personalities and the courage to fight for what was right. Something in those characters lived within her, as well, and she wanted to bring it out. Little did she know, such inner strength and courage would be a key to her survival in the years to come.

The American movies inspired Asmaa to seek personal growth and independence, but not so much that it caused her problems in Syria's male-dominated culture. She simply asked her husband for permission to attend school and promised that her education wouldn't interfere with her duties as a housewife. He agreed, and she finished high school, earned a college degree and, in 2011, began working on her Master's Degree in Library Science.

That same year, however, civil war erupted throughout Syria. The peaceful homeland Asmaa knew—a melting pot of ideologies and religions and a place she dearly loved—was ripped apart. Multiple religious and political factions within the country began fighting each other, many of them drawing support from foreign sources. The destruction has been deep and wide, the cost beyond measure. Tens of thousands of people have died in the war, and millions of families have been displaced.

After her marriage, Asmaa moved with her husband to Madyara on the outskirts of Damascus. When war broke out, her husband, a doctor, was abducted and killed. Then her sons were kidnapped and returned only after her father paid a ransom. Fearing for her life and the safety of her children, she went to her parents' home and asked for money so she and her sons could leave the country.

Soon thereafter, they crossed the border into Jordan and made their way to Egypt, where she expected to settle and raise her family. As a single mother in that culture, however, she found little help or protection, so, after two years in Egypt, she applied for refugee status.

"I had a lot of people who were harassing me as a single woman without a husband," she said. "People steal my money; they steal my wallet. I had to complain and ask for protection."

The United Nations' refugee agency (the UNHCR) deemed Asmaa a "woman at risk" and began helping her find a new home in a new country. Resettlement often takes 18-24 months, but Asmaa and her children moved quickly through the system. When she was told they would be resettled in America, they had just one week to prepare for their move.

Most refugees are settled into cities where they have existing family ties or, if they have no ties, in areas where there already are people from their homeland. That wasn't the case for Asmaa. When she and her teenage sons stepped of the airplane in November 2014, they became the first Syrian refugees placed in Boise, Idaho. The only information she had about Boise came from an American friend in Egypt, who told her to expect "snow and potatoes."

Boise is more than potatoes and snow, of course. It's a city with more than 200,000 people. But when Asmaa arrived, the census data showed that nearly than 90 percent of those people were white and only about 10 percent of the families were headed by a single-mother.[2] Most of the residents, nearly 60 percent, did not affiliate with any religion, but of those who did, fewer than 1 percent were Muslim.[3]

A culture clash seemed inevitable. This wasn't the glamourized America she'd seen in the movies, and many Americans viewed Syrian refugees with suspicion. The extreme violence of the Syrian civil war made regular appearances on the nightly news. And some of the groups fighting for control held the extremist view that produced terroristic actions, sometimes aimed at Americans. There was growing concern that along with the hurting and needy, would-be terrorists might slip through the vetting process and infiltrate America's heartland.

Asmaa seemed like an unlikely candidate to be a terrorist, but as Hashimoto said in the movie, *Little Boy,* she wore the face of the enemy. So she looked for simple ways to ease the tensions and address the fears she saw in the faces around her.

"Because I was the first one here from my country, there's no community for me," she said. "They don't smile at me and sometimes they say bad words to me. But for me, I don't care. I just want myself and my children to be safe. So I keep smiling at people so they know that I will not hurt them."

At first, she would say a few words in English, practicing what she'd learned from the movies. As she built a few relationships, she addressed more specific concerns—like the one from a woman who had heard Muslim women hid bombs under their head scarves. She simply assured the woman that she would be the first to die from such a bomb and that she wasn't ready to die. Then she offered to let the woman touch her hair.

She also was surprised to hear the misconceptions many people had about Syria.

"People ask me if Syria is in the desert," she said. "No! Syria is green mountains, it's not in the desert. Do they think that we don't have a car and that we ride the camel? I don't blame them, but from my perspective, I believe that the American people are very well-educated, so when somebody asks me if Syria is close to India, I have to say, 'No, Syria is not close to India. Syria is in the Middle East.'"

Asmaa turns those types of misunderstandings into opportunities to promote understanding about her country and about refugees.

"When people ask me a lot of questions, I understand that they don't understand anything about refugees," she said. "I need people to understand the process. For me, I feel like this is my job to get people to understand. I'm here to represent my country, too."

PERIODS OF ADJUSTMENT

Asmaa's two sons didn't grow up watching American movies, so they didn't speak any English when the family arrived
in Boise. They are adjusting, she said, to both the language
and the culture, but it's not always easy.

In February 2016, her younger son, 16 at the time, was
the victim of an assault while he was in downtown Boise. A
25-year-old man was later charged with two felony counts
of malicious harassment. According to the *Idaho Statesman*,
"The charging document asserts the victim was struck 'because of his race, color, religion, ancestry, and/or national
origin.'"

The assault didn't become public until months later.

"To build a new life here is not easy, especially for young
people," Asmaa told the *Statesman*. "At this age, a teenager—everything changed in his life in one day."[4]

Asmaa told her son not to live in fear, always to tell
people who ask that he's Muslim, and "to be a good Muslim
to let people like you."[5]

That's been her approach all along.

Asmaa now works for the Agency for New Americans, a
private non-profit organization in Boise that helped her get
settled and helps other refugees move toward self-sufficien-
cy. It provides skills training, education, and other support
to refugees.

"I love my job because I'm working with refugees, and
because I'm a refugee, I understand exactly what they need
and what they want," she said. "It's challenging work because you're dealing with a lot of trauma, but there are fun
parts, too."

Asmaa is part of a wave of refugee population growth in Idaho. From 2004 to 2014, the state took in more than 6,000 new refugees, most of them from Africa, the Near East, or South Asia.[6] Asmaa and her sons were the first Syrians to resettle in Boise, but by 2016 more than 20 other families had joined them.

At times, the tensions can rise with the culture clashes, but Asmaa remains hopeful. She plans to return to school and pursue a Master's Degree in Psychology, then teach at a university. If things go well, she hopes to attain her green card so she can travel to Jordan or Lebanon to see her family. But she never expects to return to Syria.

In the meantime, she's doing her best to adjust to her new life in America and help anyone she meets separate the truth from the stereotypes.

"I dream about peace around the world," she said. "I feel safe here. I know not all the people love me, but I don't care. I just want to smile and make everyone be my friend. I love this country, and I want to stay in this country and let this country be proud of me and proud of my kids."

Mustafa Dogan

*Mustafa Dogan helped bring Greek yogurt—
and jobs—to America.*

"We need to reduce the sugar from 28 grams to 13 grams." For one of the first English sentences Mustafa Dogan uttered upon his arrival in America, he may as well have spoken blasphemy. Everyone snickered and said it wouldn't fly in the sugarcoated culture of the U.S. of A. Mustafa, in his quest to engineer the first successful brand of Greek yogurt in America, would not waver. "13 grams of sugar will be an afterthought after this country tastes the protein-rich, low-fat, flavorful yogurt we are about to develop." Little did anyone know that in a matter of just a few years, Mustafa would sweeten the U.S. yogurt eating culture, creating a Greek yogurt formula that cut out half the sugar, while putting an exponent on profits.

Mustafa Dogan came to America knowing a lot about culture. While most of the world would rather forget the choices made in grades 9-12, Mustafa views his high school as the Cape Canaveral that launched his career. Born and raised in Turkey, he was fortunate enough to attend a special four-year program at Mehmet Rüstü Uzel, a chemistry-intense vocational high school in Ankara, where he learned the science specifically focused on working with milk cultures. The middle child of a large Turkish family, he was used to working overtime to stand out in the crowd. His training was so thorough, and he established himself as such a keen student, that he entered the workforce directly out of high school. He was hired as a lab technician for the Turkish Gov-

ernment, Agricultural Department. Within three months, Mustafa was in charge of a lab that analyzed the microbiological characteristics of pasteurized milk products. For the next 20 years, Mustafa would move between four separate Turkish companies, managing processing plants and labs for companies that dealt with dairy product manufacturing. While America was launching its "Got Milk" advertising campaign in the 90s, Mustafa was establishing himself as the only one in Turkey who *got milk cultures*. Mustafa knew dairy, and in particular, he knew yogurt, and the process of fermenting milk with bacterial cultures. Over these years, he had perfected the production of Greek yogurt, which includes a process of straining the whey out of the product, resulting in a denser, protein rich product. "America is just learning how to culture dairy products," Mustafa commented, years after he brought the process to the United States.

During the time that Mustafa was cutting his teeth in some of the biggest processing plants in Turkey, another young Turkish immigrant to America, Hamdi Ulukaya, began looking for someone with expertise to create Greek yogurt at the dairy factory he had purchased in upstate New York. Tired of the sweet, watered-down yogurt found in America, Ulukaya traveled back to Turkey to find the best yogurt maker to join him in starting a brand new market in America. He was led immediately to Mustafa, who he learned had the most expansive reputation in the industry. Ulukaya explained his vision to Mustafa, and valuing the opportunity for the wife and two children in his family, Mustafa packed up his Turkish life and moved to America to become one of the first employees of Chobani. Chobani, a derivative of the Turkish word for *shepherd*, guided Mustafa's path from the moment his feet touched American soil. Once establishing his family in a home and quality American school, he worked night and day with Ulukaya perfecting the recipe for this new yogurt. He experimented with hundreds of different bacterial cultures until they settled on a special culture band formation that remains the secret to Chobani's perfect cup of yogurt. Mustafa held the title of Yogurt Master, and at the height of Chobani's production, tasted up to four pounds of yogurt a day, ensuring strict quality control measures during the continuing expansion.

At a time in America where Greek yogurt was only manufactured by one other company and had a paltry market share of 2 percent, by 2013 Chobani had grown to 3,000 employees and Greek yogurt captured 36 percent market share of a $6.5 billion industry. The ancillary impact on agriculture was remarkable. The growing need for dairy products and fresh fruit produced in America reinvigorated the agricultural endeavors nationwide. In 2011, Chobani had outgrown the New York plant, and with the support of the Governor of Idaho, opened the largest yogurt plant in the world in the city of Twin Falls. As the third largest dairy producer in the United States, Idaho was attracted to the Chobani business model and the enormous need for quality, local dairy products. At a time when Idaho was becoming a more prominent host state for the United States refugee absorption efforts, Chobani also became a major employer with a home for refugee workers.

In this dynamic U.S. market, it didn't take long for other yogurt companies to pursue their own cup of the Greek yogurt market share. Competitors were clamoring to get Mustafa's attention to assist them in creating their own version of Greek yogurt. In 2007-2008, Stonyfield farms and Oikos both decided to process their own Greek yogurt and Oikos asked Mustafa to assist them through the use of the Chobani plant in New York. With his reputation growing in America as well, Mustafa decided to branch out and purchase his own plant in Michigan in 2014. The yogurt world had exploded in upstate New York, and sensing a climate of product saturation, he felt it was time to move his family further west and start exploring other markets and products. Now acclimated to life in America, his family was eager to continue the adventure. Mustafa's oldest son had followed in his dad's footsteps, gone to an agricultural-focused university and was on the fast track to plant management. His younger son, a seventh grader, was enjoying his American education in middle school, and his wife, at 34 years old, went to college, learned English, and was employed as a medical transcriber while taking more accounting classes.

With his family on firm ground, Mustafa decided to open his own business and test his entrepreneurial skills. Now involved in worldwide consulting, with their hands in a coffee company and a manufacturing plant, Mustafa along with Ulukaya are looking for their next business adventure. His new passion is coffee—offering a "latte in a can" through a progressive coffee company headquartered in Philadelphia. His chemist brain at work, he is exploring ways to maintain the consistency of a latte, preserved, and served in a can. This product is already offered in Whole Foods Market, amongst other outlets. In a few years, when his youngest son is in high school and asks him why he needs to take high school chemistry, Mustafa plans to sit him down at the kitchen table, with a cup of yogurt and a can of coffee, and talk about high school culture.

FINAL THOUGHTS

By Mark Russell

I honestly believe the United States of America is the greatest government in the history of the world. But we are not perfect and we never have been.

The Founding Fathers were an intelligent and wise group of men, but in hindsight we see several grievous errors in the process. Slavery was tolerated or even promoted. Native American Indians were persecuted. Women were not allowed to vote. However, over the process of time, we as a nation, have made corrections in these areas. The corrections have been slow at times and in many ways the process is not complete. But I am convinced that one important action in the early years of our nation has enabled us to progress in the right direction over the centuries and that is the First Amendment:

> Congress shall make no law respecting an establishment of religion, or prohibiting the free exercise thereof; or abridging the freedom of speech, or of the press; or the right of the people peaceably to assemble, and to petition the Government for a redress of grievances.

Freedom of religion is a foundational principle of our country and our most powerful mechanism for self-correction. It is also why the original European immigrants came here. A small religious group outside of the cultural mainstream needed a place to practice their religion without persecution.

To continue to progress as a nation, we must continue to defend freedom of religion and freedom of speech in every case. Not to do so is to undermine our own rights. Those who do not defend religious freedom will be sorry when the tide turns and they are no longer in the majority.

In our current cultural situation, at first glance some people may see some logic to temporarily banning Muslims from entering the country. The argument goes that they are coming from challenging parts of the world and terrorists can sneak in as a part of the group. Banning the entire group, they say, greatly reduces the odds of terrorist infiltration. But the unintended consequences of such an approach would be devastating.

While this kind of profiling is unconstitutional, it is also counterproductive. It creates a system of fear whereby stereotypes and stories brewed from the imagination are the downfall in our relationship with Muslims. Not the Muslims themselves.

Isolation also escalates tensions and deepens the narrative of the terrorists. We need to offer an alternative narrative. One that does not have a particular religion (Islam) at war against a people (The West), but one that shows that, at least in the United States of America, we believe in the power of diversity and inclusion, and the most fundamental and important way we need to do that is through freedom of religion and freedom of speech.

As one who grew up in the Deep South, but after the Civil Rights Era of the 1960s, I've wondered to myself, what I would have done in the 60s? Would I have put myself and my reputation on the line for what I believe was right? Would I have identified myself with the work and leadership of Dr. Martin Luther King?

The situation and circumstances are much different now, but we are all facing a question and history will judge us by how we answer it. Will we do what is right even when there is pressure to the contrary?

THE ILLEGAL IMMIGRANT

INTRODUCTION

By Dick Gephardt

Not all immigrants to America come in pursuit of a dream. Some, in fact, arrive by no choice of their own, perhaps even reluctantly. In many cases, their parents make the decision and they, as children, live with it.

What they make of this twist in their journey, of course, is up to them.

Some soar to great heights, others stumble along the path.

Angie Rodriguez has witnessed both the joy and the heartache in the lives of such immigrants.

Angie was born in Dallas, but her two older brothers were born in Mexico because her grandfather had insisted that they be Mexican citizens. After her brothers' births her family immediately returned to America and her brothers, like her, were fully indoctrinated into American culture. It was all they knew.

When one brother ran afoul of the law, he was stripped of his legal status and deported to Mexico—the country on his birth certificate but a country he didn't know. He was a stranger in his own land.

Angie's husband, on the other hand, took a different course. He was a teenager when his parents brought him to Dallas from Mexico and told him they weren't going back. He struggled to understand why his life had been uprooted and replanted in the red clay of Texas. But once he found his why, Rolando Rodriguez quickly found his way.

Rolando Rodriguez

When Rolando Rodriguez found his why in America, he soon began to find his way.

A well-known story in the Bible tells of a man who tried his best to avoid the assignment God had given him. God told him to leave his homeland and preach in a foreign country; instead, the man ran away. More accurately, he sailed away. He bought a ticket, got on a boat, and headed the other direction.

You might know what happened next: God wrecked the ship and the man's plans. When the man confessed that his disobedience to God had caused the ship's calamity, the sailors threw him overboard, and the seas calmed. A large fish—some say a whale—then swallowed the man and spit him out three days later on the shores of the very country where God had told him to go preach.

Rolando Rodriguez isn't exactly a modern Jonah. But as the senior pastor of Erez Baptist Church in Duncanville, Texas and the director of Hispanic Ministries for the Baptist General Convention of Texas, he is preaching in a land he arrived in reluctantly and that he never expected to call home.

You see, Rolando was more of an "import" to America than an immigrant. And it wasn't until he fully understood *why* God had brought him to this country that he began to find his way in it.

Rolando was 15 in December, 1979 when his mother brought him to Dallas for what he thought was a two-week visit over Christmas break. His father, Pedro Rodriguez, had

been using temporary visas to work in the U.S. as a diesel mechanic since the 1960s. Rolando's parents had eight sons, and the older siblings also were working in Texas. They worked hard, lived simply, and regularly sent money to their family in Mexico.

Rolando was part of that family in Mexico. He and the rest of his brothers lived with their mother in Reynosa, Mexico, a border town just west of Brownsville, Texas.

Reynosa was home to Rolando, and he had no desire to leave. He was an above average student in his school and an outgoing teenager who enjoyed playing soccer and spending time with his friends. Life as he knew it was good. So he expected to show up in Dallas, spend time with his dad and other family members, and then return to his home—and his life.

Then his father sat Rolando and his brothers down for a reality check: You aren't going back, he told them.

"We never dreamed of coming to the United States," Rolando said. "Once we were here, we had no say in it. They decided the whole family is here, so we might as well stay. That was the beginning of our journey in the United States."

That journey has seen Rolando go from a teenager visiting his family legally to an illegal alien afraid to leave his home to a hard-working permanent resident to an influential pastor and U.S. citizen.

His story reflects the power of hard work, the importance of education, and value of finding and following a purpose.

CHECKING THE RADAR

Pedro Rodriguez came to America for the same reason many other immigrants come: to work. And that's what he expected of his sons, including Rolando.

"He told us to find a job, and I did for a few months," Rolando said. "He was saying this is why we came here: to work and make money. Education was not on his radar."

Education, however, was on Rolando's mother's radar. She insisted that he and his other three school-aged brothers enroll in classes. Suddenly Rolando found himself in a high school with teachers and classmates who mostly spoke a different language. And because his temporary visa had expired, he no longer could move freely throughout the community.

"I remember like it was yesterday," he said. "We didn't argue about being here, because, in our family, you didn't argue with our dad. But my brothers and I struggled with it. We were just coming for a couple of weeks. Just Christmas break. We didn't bring anything other than our clothes for two weeks. We left behind everything. It was not much, but it was *our* things, *our* friends, *our* school."

In the early 1980s, there weren't many English as Second Language (ESL) programs, so the biggest barrier Rolando faced was communication. He went right into the same classes as everyone else, and he quickly went from an above-average student in Mexico to a student who struggled to get by at Sunset High School in Dallas.

"They assumed it's your problem if you don't understand," he said. "I still have my transcript from high school, and it's pretty embarrassing. I graduated because all you needed was a D to graduate. I had many classes I passed with just a 60—a D. They didn't have tests you had to pass to graduate like they do now, so I was blessed. I don't think I could have done it."

After school each day, Rolando no longer went to the soccer fields to play with friends or to a part-time job to earn money for the family. He went to the one-bedroom duplex that he and his six siblings called home, and he stayed there.

"If you went out," he said, "you were always thinking immigration is going to pick you up. In the 80s, the border patrol would block the streets. If you didn't have your documents, they would take you."

Those first three years, however, became the most important in Rolando's life, even if he didn't realize it at the time. First, he finished high school and learned enough English to communicate and to make a living. Second, he met the girl who would become his wife. And, third, he found the purpose that would shape his life.

His future wife and his lifelong purpose were found in the same place: *Primera Iglesia Bautista* Church in Oak Cliff, Texas.

FINDING A PARTNER

Angie Moreno was just 14 when, on September 25, 1983, she joined a Sunday School class that included the 17-year-old Rolando. Her parents had immigrated to America as married teenagers. They returned to Mexico for the birth of her older brothers, but she was born in Dallas. She embraced the culture and the English language, and she found church and school to be places of refuge from her troubled family.

She attended the same school as Rolando, but they met and became friends at church.

"I came into a Sunday School class full of young men and very few young women," she said. "But I was not looking for a boyfriend. Far from it, I did not want anything to do with boys. I grew up in a dysfunctional home, and I had no plans for marriage. I was especially not interested in Mexicans. From what I saw in the Mexican culture, they were drunks, abusive, and unfaithful. I wanted and was praying for a Godly man who loved the Lord with all of his heart. I never thought I could find that in a Hispanic guy. But I was wrong."

Despite her apprehensions, Angie and Rolando soon became friends and played a key role in helping each other with their language skills. Even though Angie's parents were first-generation immigrants from Mexico, she spoke very little Spanish and had intentionally distanced herself from the Mexican culture.

"Her parents worked from 5 in the morning until 5 at night," Rolando said. "They would get something to eat and go to sleep. So she didn't know a lot of Spanish, and I didn't know English. I told her, 'I'm going to teach you Spanish and you're going to teach me English.' I would speak to her in English and she would speak to me in Spanish. Now she is excellent in Spanish."

Angie was more concerned with teaching Rolando the difference between "there" and "their" than she was about his legal status in America. "I really didn't even know what it was until I had already fallen head over heels for him," she said. By that time, Rolando already had begun the process of securing his permanent resident status.

He was one of an estimated 2 million immigrants who went from illegal to legal by taking advantage of the Simpson-Mazzoli Act, a bipartisan immigration reform bill that Congress passed in 1986. To qualify, he had to prove he had no criminal convictions, that he had been in the country since before January 1, 1982, and that he had a basic knowledge of U.S. history, government, and the English language.

Rolando, of course, met all the qualifications and finally moved out of the shadows.

Fewer than two years later, he and Angie were married.

"We had a pretty healthy friendship for almost five years," he said. "Our relationship was around church. That made our relationship healthy."

Once he was married, Rolando knew he never wanted to leave the United States. But he went more than 20 years before becoming a U.S. citizen.

"You can apply after five years, but I didn't," he said. "In those days, there was a lot of misunderstanding, a lot of misinformation. They would say if you get your U.S. citizenship you lose all your rights in Mexico. Things like that. I didn't think it was necessary. I didn't know all the benefits of becoming a U.S. citizen."

One benefit he soon discovered involved international travel. When Rolando traveled outside the U.S., getting in and out always proved complicated. Angie eventually refused to travel with him until he became a citizen. She filled out the paperwork for him several times, but it wasn't until 2008, with the help of a friend, that he completed the process.

"Once he became a citizen," Angie said, "we began to travel together again."

By that time, Rolando had become well-established as a pastor in the Dallas area. That part of their journey had begun shortly after he and Angie were married, and that's when Rolando began to fully appreciate his mother's decision to keep him in school when he first arrived in Dallas.

During his younger years, when he told his pastor that he felt called to the ministry, his pastor told him he needed to leave his job at the local factory and go back to school "if you want to serve God."

So Rolando and his new wife headed to San Antonio, where he earned a degree from the Hispanic Baptist Theological Seminary (now the Baptist University of the Americas). He later earned a master's degree from Dallas Baptist University and is finishing work on his doctorate through Midwestern Baptist Theological Seminary.

Rolando worked as an associate pastor for the church in Dallas that sent him to San Antonio, and later spent 17 years as its senior pastor. By that time, the Hispanic and Anglo congregations had merged into one multi-cultural church. He continues to serve as a senior pastor, but most of his work with the local church involves supporting other leaders who handle the day-to-day and week-to-week church activities.

As the director of Hispanic Ministries for the Baptist General Convention of Texas, Rolando works with around 1,100 congregations across the state—most of which are bilingual. He and Angie are on the road most weeks, sometimes for two or three weeks at a time. Their children—two biological daughters, and a son, and two adopted daughters—all are grown and are working or in college.

Rolando, of course, is passionate about education—for himself, for his children, and for all immigrants. His church has a scholarship fund to help students of all ages finish high school and attend college.

"I want to change the mindset in our culture," he said. "First generation, those who come from Mexico or another country, a big percentage of them don't come here to go to school. They come to work. We need to change that. Nothing compares with someone who receives a good education. That will change your life forever. It's my responsibility to pass that along. And not just to young people. We need to help adults, also. There are many ways we can help them. We've had people in our church in their 40s, 50s, 60s who got their GED."

THE HEART OF THE *WHY*

Education provided Rolando Rodriguez with a way forward, but he's quick to point out that his "why" was even more important.

"When you know your why, then you know your way," he said.

As a teenager, he was unable to leave the country and there was no way for him to stay here legally. So he often asked himself the most basic of life's big questions: Why am I here?

"I was trying to answer that question at 16 when someone presented the Gospel to me," he said, "and that's when I understood that this is why: God had a plan. Once I found that why, then I found my way. The thing that changed my life completely as an immigrant was my relationship with Christ. That was in 1981. I was 16. It was a God thing. God put us there for such a time as this. Now I'm 50. It's been an amazing journey."

In research for his doctorate, Rolando has found a strong connection between immigrants who have a strong faith and those who are living a stable, productive life.

"I know why," he said. "Christ is the difference. Now you have a purpose. You are not here just to make money or make a living. Now you are here to make a difference. To be a good citizen. To make an impact. It's not about you anymore. It's about others."

Luis Marioni

Luis Marioni's father knew it would take hard work to bring his family to the United States.

Luis Marioni well knows the power of the American Dream. It was instilled in him early on, by his father, Arturo Marioni, the son of an Italian immigrant to Mexico. Arturo, who was born on a small ranch in Chihuahua, Mexico, originally came to the U.S. illegally, to work as a migrant worker.

In the village of Santa Rita in Mexico, Arturo Marioni had labored hard for his family, and his entire village. He was instrumental in building both a school and a park in the village, as well as bringing in the first phone booth. His son remembers him always doing something to help others. That was his heart.

At the same time, he didn't ever give up his dream to live and work in America, desperately wanting a better life for his family.

Arturo's employer in Texas, well aware of his illegal status, knew that if for some reason he didn't show up for work, it was only because he had been caught by the border patrol. He knew he'd get there eventually. This happened numerous times over the years, as Arturo crossed back and forth across the river every two weeks in order to visit his family, before eventually bringing his wife and children to El Paso.

Luis, newly arrived in the U.S., was enrolled in the first grade in 1972. The family was happy to be all together and settling in nicely when, after a year and a half, they were suddenly deported back to Mexico. He remembers being made to repeat the first grade once he returned to Mexico, not necessarily because he was behind in school, but because he was younger than the other children.

Thankfully, and somewhat providentially, during the time the Marioni family had been living in the U.S., a younger brother was born. This brother was automatically a resident of the U.S., which, in turn, allowed Arturo to become a resident.

After a time, Arturo once again attempted to bring his family to the U.S. The family was more fortunate this time around. Luis's mother had a stepsister who had an impressive immigration story herself, and she was able to offer the family some assistance.

Romana Acosta Bañuelos was the first Hispanic U.S. Treasurer and part of President Nixon's administration in the early 1970's. A successful businesswoman who had been born in the U.S., but deported back to Mexico as a child during the Great Depression, only to return as an 18-year-old with two small children, Romana Acosta Bañuelos was more than happy to help her family members gain their American citizenship. She wrote a letter on their behalf. Not only were they allowed back into the country, but Luis, his parents and his siblings were awarded their citizenship in record time.

Once again, the entire family moved to the U.S. This time around, ironically, Luis was put into the third grade, even though he'd just completed third grade in Mexico. Repeating grades seemed to be a pattern for him.

The Marioni family, Luis, his parents and seven siblings, worked hard as new citizens. They were extremely poor and life in El Paso's projects was challenging. They were surrounded by poverty, danger, and crime. His father continued to work, now as a pastor, and raised his children to value hard work, Jesus, and an American education. Luis feels very grateful. "I owe everything that I have to my dad's drive."

Luis and his siblings have taken advantage of the fact that, as he said, "Anyone can go to school in America." The family includes two doctors, including Luis, and two pastors, as well as a host of other educated and accomplished siblings.

Luis waited to go to college, rather than going immediately after high school. He spent several years working and helping his family out financially. During this time, he worked in a health food store and became very interested in nutrition, and health in general. After a few years, he decided to go to school to pursue a doctorate degree in Chiropractic, and later earned another two two-year degrees in Clinical Nutrition and Advanced Practice in Chiropractic.

He definitely believes in the power of a college education. "A lot of people don't think that they can make it, they think being a doctor or an attorney is just for the elite or for the people who have it better, but the fact is that you can get an education here in the United States. Anybody can do it."

Luis had found great financial success being a Hispanic chiropractor in El Paso, and in 2001 was named one of the Top 20 Doctors in the state of Texas. His interest in helping people live healthy lives is evident in the work that he continues to do.

Luis Marioni is busy opening new clinics across the state of New Mexico, publishing a health-focused Hispanic magazine, planning a daycare center for special needs adults, and starting a non-profit foundation that helps kids with cancer…which he hopes to hand off to his two daughters someday.

In other words, he's working very hard, building a legacy, just as he learned from his father.

FINAL THOUGHTS

By Mark Russell

When I speak on immigration, I frequently get the question, "Are you talking about illegal or legal immigration?" As my partner, Dick Gephardt, has rightfully pointed out, we should enforce the laws of our land, but these stories also illustrate that the legality issue on immigration is not always as clear as it is in other situations.

We also have to acknowledge that we have had an inadequate system in place for decades that has disrupted families and created a situation where some people in an immediate family are legal and others are not.

Personal relationships with families in this situation frequently change people's minds as to the way things should be. I once knew a family who was ardently opposed to illegal immigration and took a hard stance of punishment with a very strong black/white viewpoint. They had a Mexican family who helped them with various tasks around the house. The husband worked as their gardener and the wife and one daughter as their housekeepers. They didn't realize that the husband was illegal and the wife and daughter legal, until one day the wife and daughter showed up by themselves and said that the husband had been deported. This one situation caused this influential family to realize that illegal immigration is not a black/white issue and that what sounds good in theory doesn't work as well when applied to the people you know and love.

Illegal immigrants are a significant part of American culture and society. We need to find a just and humane path forward. By getting to know them, we hope that compassion and reason will guide our decisions.

THE AMERICAN IMMIGRANT

VOLUME ONE: FINAL THOUGHTS

By Mark Russell

My wife, Laurie, and I consider ourselves quite fortunate for having lived in numerous countries. For the most part, we always have been welcomed and viewed quite positively wherever we lived. People love and are fascinated by American culture. They realized we were there to contribute to their society and economic well-being. So the reception was always good. We had it far better than most foreigners do, including those who come to America. Nevertheless, living in a foreign country comes with its own set of challenges.

Mundane tasks can become confusing. Where to shop for food. How to take public transportation. A foreigner is frequently confronted with social rules that they never know until they break them. I didn't know that I should be pushing our newborn baby in his stroller on the right-hand side of the sidewalk until I was told I was "full of sh**" for being on the left. We didn't realize that we should have our own midwife until we were in the hospital with Laurie in labor. When our two-year old daughter swallowed Drano and was in a life threatening situation, we didn't know what to do or to whom to turn.

The people who helped us along the path have a special place in our hearts, even though we probably don't fully realize everything they did for us. Having these experiences built within us a finely tuned understanding of what it means to be a foreigner and an empathy for the foreigners among us. We have sought to have real relationships with the people who have, for whatever reason, come from another country to live in ours. Many of them live in isolation. One foreigner, after three years of residence in the U.S., told Laurie that she was her only American friend. These relationships have opened our eyes not only to how much they need us to help them, similarly to how people helped us, but also to how much we need them for who they are and who they help us to become.

EPIC IMMIGRATION

The movement of people around the globe has reached epic proportions. There are an estimated 250 million immigrants around the world, 42 million of them in the United States and accounting for approximately 13 percent of our population. The U.S.-born children of immigrants almost double the total to 81 million people or 26 percent of everyone in the U.S.[1]*

---

[1] * The term "immigrants" (also known as the foreign born) refers to people residing in the United States who were not U.S. citizens at birth. This population includes naturalized citizens, lawful permanent residents (LPRs), certain legal nonimmigrants (e.g., persons on student or work visas), those admitted under refugee or asylee status, and persons illegally residing in the United States. http://www.migrationpolicy.org/programs/data-hub/charts/immigrant-population-over-time?width=1000&height=850&iframe=true

There are any number of reasons why people move from one place to the next. Throughout history, people have moved to expand an empire or to flee an expanding empire. Sometimes they are displaced due to conflict or natural disaster. Other times, they are in search of opportunity and a better life for themselves and their children.

However, the U.S., historically and currently, has been a special place for immigrants. Built on the foundation of people seeking life, liberty, and the pursuit of happiness, America has always been a place of hope for immigrants.

MOVEMENT LEADS TO CHALLENGES

Whenever people move from one location to the next, complications ensue. Discrimination and resentment oftentimes accompany the movement. In the U.S., the waves of immigration have been met on occasion with a push back. In the mid-19th century there were numerous cases of violent attacks against Catholic immigrants. In 1882, President Chester Arthur signed the Chinese Exclusion Act, effectively banning all Chinese laborers. In the early 20th century, overriding President Woodrow Wilson's veto, Congress overwhelmingly passed the 1917 Immigration Act banning "undesirables" and the "Asiatic Barred Zone Act," which banned immigrants from most Asian and Pacific Island nations.

Resistance to new arrivals is in large part a natural instinct—something readily observed in the natural world, where animals are territorial and have an obvious fear of other animals. But, as human beings in today's world, is it necessary for us to adhere to this fear of the other?

When we look at American immigrants today, we have to look at the entire balance of their contribution and engagement and ask ourselves a simple question: Are we better off with immigrants? I believe we are.

WILL IMMIGRANTS TAKE AWAY JOBS?

Criticism of immigrants comes in many forms. One frequently repeated knock is that immigrants take American jobs. But, is this true? If you view the economy as pie with only so many slices to be divided (or only so many jobs to be had), then it is easy to reach this conclusion. However, if the economy is something that can grow, more like a vineyard where you can increase the yield of grapes, and where someone toiling the ground actually helps others benefit, then maybe there is the opportunity to view it differently.

Statistically, the latter appears to be true. For every low-skilled, foreign-born laborer hired in the U.S., 4.6 native-born laborers are hired. When it comes to high-skilled labor, 2.8 native-born employees are hired for every foreign-born employee.[7] Far from taking native-born American jobs, the influx of immigrant labor consistently creates more jobs and helps the U.S. economy to stay on a desired growth trajectory. If it weren't for immigrant labor sustaining the U.S. economy, it is entirely plausible that the U.S. economy would slow, resulting in the loss of jobs for native-born Americans.

It is assumed by some that the U.S. educational system is capable of providing all of the highly-trained jobs required from the U.S. market, but the evidence suggests something to the contrary. Many critical skills are still in demand. In 2014, high-tech H-1B visas were issued within the first week they became available, illustrating our need for such workers. Furthermore, these workers are significantly adding to our job base, rather than taking away from it. A foreign-born graduate with a STEM (Science, Technology, Engineering, and Mathematics) degree is associated with an additional 2.6 jobs for native-born Americans.[8] Astonishingly, 50 percent of Silicon Valley startups are founded by foreign-born residents. Between 1995 and 2005, these companies created 450,000 U.S. jobs and generated $52 billion in sales.[9]

Far from taking jobs, immigrants are creating them.

WILL IMMIGRANTS INCREASE CRIME?

Another reproof is that immigrants are often coming from trying circumstances and bring those challenges with them, resulting in an increase in crime. One of the fears that law-abiding, native-born Americans have is that with the importation of people comes a boatload of problems.

But recent research indicates the exact opposite. Native-born citizens are more prone to criminal activity than foreign-born residents. Drs. Walter Ewing, Daniel Martinez, and Rubén Rumbaut released their research findings, which indicated the following:[10]

- Higher immigration is associated with lower crime rates.

The research shows that between 1990 and 2013, the foreign-born share of the U.S. population grew from 7.9 percent to 13.1 percent, but FBI data indicate that the violent crime rate declined 48 percent—which included falling rates of aggravated assault, robbery, rape, and murder.

Likewise, the property crime rate fell 41 percent, including declining rates of motor vehicle theft, larceny/robbery, and burglary.

- Immigrants are less likely than the native-born to be behind bars and to engage in criminal behavior.

Roughly 1.6 percent of immigrant males age 18-39 are incarcerated, compared to 3.3 percent of the native-born. These findings are consistent with data from the 1980, 1990, and 2000 censuses. In each of those decades, the incarceration rates of the native-born were anywhere from two to five times higher than that of immigrants.

In 2010, less-educated native-born men aged 18-39 had an incarceration rate of 10.7 percent—more than triple the 2.8 percentage rate among foreign-born Mexican men. Wide ranging studies with various methodologies demonstrate that immigrants are less likely than the native-born to engage in either violent or nonviolent "antisocial" behaviors; that immigrants are less likely than the native-born to be repeat offenders among "high-risk" adolescents; and that immigrant youth who were students in U.S. middle and high schools in the mid-1990s and are now young adults have among the lowest delinquency rates of all young people. [11]

THE POPULATION REALITY

Immigrants are not without their challenges, but neither are native-born Americans or any group of people for that matter. These findings support the experiences of the vast majority of Americans (native and foreign born) that we know.

Over the years, we have intentionally sought to develop relationships with immigrant Americans and their stories have ranged from sensational to mundane. Regardless, 99 percent of them have been inspirational, hearing their journeys to America, the land of opportunity, and seeking an overwhelmingly better life for their children.

Statistics and debate have their place. But they never take the place of real relationships with real people. The stories in this book are about the real people who make up the American immigrant, reminding us that we have always been a place of hope, a nation of immigrants and that together we create a better country, safer, freer, and more prosperous.

Due to the enormous number of immigrants in America, we all have regular contact with immigrants or we are ourselves an immigrant. We would love to hear your stories as well. The immigrants you know. The immigrants you are. Submit your stories at https://elevatepub.com/american-immigrant/.

CITATIONS

[1] http://www.chicagotribune.com/entertainment/theater/news/ct-lin-manuel-miranda-hamilton-commencement-speech-20160516-story.html

[2] http://factfinder.census.gov/faces/nav/jsf/pages/community_facts.xhtml

[3] http://www.city-data.com/city/Boise-City-Idaho.html

[4] "Distorted Idaho report recalls real attack for Boise Syrian refugee," by Bill Dentzer, the *Idaho Statesman*, June 22, 2016

[5] ibid

[6] http://www.idahorefugees.org/refugees-in-idaho.html

[7] http://www.hoover.org/sites/default/files/hoover_immigration_fact_sheet.pdf

[8] ibid

[9] http://papers.ssrn.com/sol3/papers.cfm?abstract_id=990152

[10] *Criminalization of immigration in The United States*. Walter A. Ewing, Ph.D., Daniel E. Martínez, Ph.D., and Rubén G. Rumbaut, Ph.D. American Immigration Council. Special Report. July 2015 available at http://immigrationpolicy.org/sites/default/files/docs/the_criminalization_of_immigration_in_the_united_states_final.pdf

[11] ibid

ACKNOWLEDGMENTS

DICK GEPHARDT:

To Matt and Tricia Gephardt for their shared belief in the importance of immigration in shaping America's history and defining its future, and for their work in helping me make this book series a reality.

MARK RUSSELL:

To my wife, Laurie Deaton Russell, for her love of diversity and seeing the beauty of all people, and to our foreign-born children, Noah and Anastasia, whose love for culture and others is an inspiration.

And to our writers and researchers Stephen Caldwell, Mindy Bach and Jana Good.

ABOUT THE AUTHORS

HONORABLE RICHARD "DICK" GEPHARDT is an American politician who served as a United States Representative from Missouri from 1977 to 2005. A member of the Democratic Party, he was House Majority Leader from 1989 to 1995 and Minority Leader from 1995 to 2003. Since his retirement from politics, Dick has served as President and CEO of Gephardt Group. He enjoys strong bipartisan relationships in the House of Representatives, serves as a trusted adviser to senior officials in the Administration and on Capitol Hill, and has counseled numerous CEOs during negotiations with labor. He has been featured in national publications, including *The New York Times, The Wall Street Journal, The Washington Post, National Journal, Roll Call, The Hill* and *Time*.

MARK L. RUSSELL is the Co-Founder and CEO of Russell Media Corporation and Elevate Publishing. A long-time advocate of international human rights, Dr. Mark Russell has worked in economic development initiatives around the world and in the United States. A traveler to over 70 countries and an author of over 70 publications, Mark is passionate about clearly communicating stories and ideas that add to the beauty and diversity of humanity. A strategic adviser to CEOs and government officials, Mark and his company have been featured in numerous national publications. He lives in Boise, Idaho with his wife, Laurie, and their two children.

elevate
publishing

DELIVERING TRANSFORMATIVE MESSAGES
TO THE WORLD

Visit www.elevatepub.com for our latest offerings.